BERLITZ®

GERMAN
FOR TRAVELLERS

By the staff of Editions Berlitz

Library of Congress Catalog Card Number: 74-1976

First revised edition
8th printing 1981

Printed in Switzerland

Editions Berlitz
1, avenue des Jordils
1000 Lausanne 6, Switzerland

Preface

In preparing this complete revision of *German for Travellers,* we took into consideration a wealth of suggestions and criticisms received by phrase-book users around the world. As a result, this new edition features:

a) a complete phonetic transcription throughout indicating the pronunciation of all words and phrases you'll need to know on your trip

b) special sections showing the replies your listener might give to you. Just hand him the book and let him point to the appropriate phrase. This is especially practical in certain difficult situations (doctor, garage mechanic, etc.).

c) a complete revision of the section on Eating Out to make it even more useful in a restaurant. Austrian and German Swiss items have been included, too.

d) a tipping chart and a more comprehensive reference section in the back of the book.

These are new features. They complement what has become the world's most popular phrase-book series, helping you with:

* all the phrases and supplementary vocabulary you'll need on your trip
* a wide variety of tourist and travel facts, tips and useful information
* audio aids in the form of cassettes, cartridges and LP records
* quick reference through colour coding. The major features of the contents are on the back cover. A complete index is found inside.

These are just a few of the practical advantages. In addition, the book will prove a valuable introduction to life in Germany, Austria and Switzerland.

There's a comprehensive section on Eating Out, giving translations and explanations for practically anything one would find on a German menu; there's a complete Shopping Guide that will enable you to obtain virtually anything you want.

Trouble with the car? Turn to the mechanic's manual with its dual-language terms. Feeling ill? Our medical section provides the most rapid communication possible between you and the doctor.

To make the most of *German for Travellers,* we suggest that you start with the "Guide to Pronunciation". Then go on to "Some Basic Expressions". This not only gives you a minimum vocabulary: it helps you to pronounce the language.

We're particularly grateful to Mrs. C.A. Carl-Sime and Miss Sylvia Reul for their help in the preparation of this book and to Dr. T.J.A. Bennett who devised the phonetic transcription. We also wish to thank the German Central Tourist Association for its assistance.

We shall be very pleased to receive any comments, criticisms and suggestions that you think may help us in preparing future editions.

Thank you. Have a good trip.

Throughout this book, the symbols illustrated here indicate small sections where phrases have been compiled that your foreign listener might like to say to *you.* If you don't understand him, give him the book and let him point to the phrase in his language. The English translation is just beside it.

Basic Grammar

Here is the briefest possible outline of some essential features of German grammar.

Articles

All nouns in German are either masculine, feminine or neuter, and they are classified by the article which precedes them.

1. **Definite article** (the):

			Plural:
masc.	*der* **Mann**	the man	*die* **Männer**
fem.	*die* **Frau**	the woman	*die* **Frauen**
neut.	*das* **Kind**	the child	*die* **Kinder**

2. **Indefinite article** (a/an):

masc.	*ein* **Zug**	a train
fem.	*eine* **Reise**	a trip
neut.	*ein* **Flugzeug**	a plane

3. **Declension:** See under nouns below.

Nouns

1. All nouns are written with a capital letter.

2. **Declension:** According to their use in the sentence, German nouns change their endings. Since articles and modifying adjectives undergo related changes, the tables below show the declension of all three parts of speech.

	masc. sing.	masc. plur.
subject	**der reiche Mann**	**die reichen Männer**
possessive	**des reichen Mannes**	**der reichen Männer**
direct object	**den reichen Mann**	**die reichen Männer**
indirect object	**dem reichen Mann**	**den reichen Männern**

	fem. sing.	fem. plur.
subject	**die schöne Frau**	**die schönen Frauen**
possessive	**der schönen Frau**	**der schönen Frauen**
direct object	**die schöne Frau**	**die schönen Frauen**
indirect object	**der schönen Frau**	**den schönen Frauen**

	neuter sing.	neuter plur.
subject	**das kleine Kind**	**die kleinen Kinder**
possessive	**des kleinen Kindes**	**der kleinen Kinder**
direct object	**das kleine Kind**	**die kleinen Kinder**
indirect object	**dem kleinen Kind**	**den kleinen Kindern**

Adjectives

1. See above. However, the declensions shown are for an adjective used in conjunction with the definite article. Different endings are used for adjectives with the indefinite article or without an article.

2. As can be seen from the above, the position of adjectives within the sentence is similar to English usage.

3. **Demonstrative adjectives:**

	masc.	fem.	neut.	plur.
this	**dieser**	**diese**	**dieses**	**diese**
that	**jener**	**jene**	**jenes**	**jene**

4. **Possessive adjectives:** These agree in number and gender with the noun they modify, i.e., with the thing possessed and not the possessor. They are declined like **der, die, das**.

Note that **Ihr** meaning "your" in the polite form is capitalized.

GRAMMAR

	masc. or neut.	fem. or plur.
my	**mein**	**meine**
your	**dein**	**deine**
his / its	**sein**	**seine**
her	**ihr**	**ihre**
our	**unser**	**unsere**
your	**euer**	**eure**
their	**ihr**	**ihre**
your (pol.)	**Ihr**	**Ihre**

5. **Comparatives and superlatives:** These are formed by adding **-er (-r)** and **-est (-st)** respectively, very often together with an *Umlaut*

alt (old)
älter (older)
ältest (oldest)

kurz (short)
kürzer (shorter)
kürzest (shortest)

They are regularly declined:

ein längeres Kleid — a longer dress
der kürzeste Weg — the shortest way

Adverbs

Many adjectives are used in their undeclined form as adverbs.

schnell — quick, quickly
gut — good, well

There are a few irregularities:

glücklich – glücklicherweise — happy–happily
anders — differently
besonders — especially
gleichfalls — as well, (the) same

Viel indicates quantity and **sehr** intensity:

Er arbeitet viel. — He works a lot.
Er ist sehr müde. — He's very tired.

Personal pronouns

	subject	direct object	indirect object
I	**ich**	**mich**	**mir**
you	**du**	**dich**	**dir**
he	**er**	**ihn**	**ihm**
she	**sie**	**sie**	**ihr**
it	**es**	**es**	**ihm**
we	**wir**	**uns**	**uns**
you	**ihr**	**euch**	**euch**
they	**sie**	**sie**	**ihnen**
you	**Sie**	**Sie**	**Ihnen**

Note: There are two forms for "you" in German: **du** (plur.: **ihr**) is used when talking to relatives, close friends and children (and between young people); **Sie** is used in all other cases. **Sie** is written with a capital S. The verb has the same form as that of the 3rd person plural.

Verbs

Here we are concerned only with the infinitive, the present tense, and the imperative.

Learn these two important **auxiliary verbs:**

sein (to be)

ich bin (I am)
du bist (you are)
er, sie, es ist (he, she, it is)
wir sind (we are)
ihr seid (you are)
sie sind (they are)
Sie sind (you are)

haben (to have)

ich habe (I have)
du hast (you have)
er, sie, es hat (he, she, it has)
wir haben (we have)
ihr habt (you have)
sie haben (they have)
Sie haben (you have)

The infinitive of practically all verbs ends in **-en**. Here are the endings for the present tense:

ich lieb*e*	I love
du lieb*st*	you love
er, sie, es lieb*t*	he, she, it loves
wir lieb*en*	we love
ihr lieb*t*	you love
sie, Sie lieb*en*	they, you love

Here are four useful irregular verbs in the present tense:

	können (to be able)	**gehen** (to go)	**sehen** (to see)	**tun** (to do)
ich	**kann**	**gehe**	**sehe**	**tue**
du	**kannst**	**gehst**	**siehst**	**tust**
er / sie / es	**kann**	**geht**	**sieht**	**tut**
wir	**können**	**gehen**	**sehen**	**tun**
ihr	**könnt**	**geht**	**seht**	**tut**
sie / Sie	**können**	**gehen**	**sehen**	**tun**

For both regular and irregular verbs, the **imperative** is formed by reversing the order of the verb and the personal pronoun.

Gehen wir! Let's go!
Gehen Sie! Go!

Negatives

Negatives are formed with **nicht**.

Er ist nicht hier. He is not here.

Questions

These are formed by inverting the subject and the verb (putting the verb first, the subject second).

Sprechen Sie Englisch? Do you speak English?

Guide to pronunciation

This and the following chapter are intended to make you familiar with the phonetic transcription we have devised and to help you get used to the sounds of German.

As a minimum vocabulary for your trip, we've selected a number of basic words and phrases under the title "Some Basic Expressions" (pages 15–21).

You'll find the pronunciation of the German letters and sounds explained below, as well as the symbols we're using for them in the transcriptions.

The imitated pronunciation should be read as if it were English; the symbols for sounds that don't exist in English should, however, be pronounced as described in the appropriate section of the following guide. Of course, the sounds of any two languages are never exactly the same; but if you follow carefully the indications supplied here, you'll have no difficulty in reading our transcriptions in such a way as to make yourself understood.

In the transcriptions, letters shown in bold print should be read with more stress (louder) than the others.

Consonants

Letter	Approximate pronunciation	Symbol	Example	
f, h, k, l, m, n, p, t, x	normally pronounced as in English			
b	1) at the end of a word or between a vowel and a consonant like **p** in **up**	p	**ab**	ahp
	2) elsewhere as in English	b	**bis**	biss

c	1) before **e**, i, **ö** and ä, like **ts** in hits	ts	**Celsius**	**tsehl**zeeuss
	2) elsewhere like **c** in cat	k	**Café**	kah**fay**
ch	1) like **ch** in Scottish **loch**	kh	**ich**	ikh
	2) sometimes, especially before s, like **k** in **kit**	k	**Wachs**	vahks
d	1) at the end of a word or between a vowel and a consonant like **t** in eat	t	**Rad**	rart
	2) elsewhere, like **d** in **do**	d	**durstig**	**door**stikh
g	1) always hard as in **go** but at the end of a word often more like **ck** in **tack**	g k	**gehen** **weg**	**gay**ern vehk
	2) when preceded by i at the end of a word like **ch** in Scottish **loch**	kh	**billig**	**bil**likh
j	like **y** in **yes**	y	**ja**	yar
qu	like **k** followed by **v** in **vat**	kv	**Quark**	kvahrk
r	generally rolled in the back of the mouth	r	**warum**	vahrum
s	1) before or between vowels like **z** in **zoo**	z	**sie**	zee
	2) before **p** and **t** at the beginning of a syllable like **sh** in **shut**	sh	**spät**	shpait
	3) elsewhere, like **s** in **sit**	s/ss	**es ist**	ehss ist
ß	always like **s** in **sit**	s/ss	**heiß**	highss
sch	like **sh** in **shut**	sh	**schnell**	shnehl
tsch	like **ch** in **chip**	ch	**deutsch**	doych
tz	like **ts** in **hits**	ts	**Platz**	plahts
v	like **f** in **for**	f	**vier**	feer
w	like **v** in **vice**	v	**wie**	vee
z	like **ts** in **hits**	ts	**zeigen**	**tsigh**gern

PRONUNCIATION

Vowels

In Germany, vowels are generally long when followed by **h** or by one consonant and short when followed by two or more consonants.

a	1) short like **u** in cut	ah	**hat**	haht
	2) long like **a** in car	ar	**Abend**	**ar**bernt
ä	1) short like **e** in let	eh	**Lärm**	lehrm
	2) long like **ai** in hair	ai	**spät**	shpait
e	1) short like **e** in let	eh	**sprechen**	**shpreh**khern
	2) long like **a** in late	ay	**gehen**	**gay**ern
	3) in unstressed syllables it's generally pronounced like **er** in other	er	**bitte**	**bit**ter
			geben	**gay**bern
i	1) short like **i** in hit	i	**bis**	biss
	2) long like **ee** in meet	ee	**ihm**	eem
ie	like **ee** in bee	ee	**hier**	heer
o	1) short like **o** in got	o	**voll**	fol
	2) long like **o** in note	oa	**ohne**	**oa**ner
ö	like **ur** in fur (long or short)	ur	**können**	**kur**nern
u	1) short like **oo** in foot	u	**Nuß**	nuss
	2) long like **oo** in moon	oo	**gut**	goot
ü	like French **u** in **une**; no English equivalent. Round your lips and try to say **ea** as in **mean**	ew	**über**	**ew**ber
y	like German **ü**	ew	**Symphonie**	zewmfoa**nee**

Diphthongs

ai, ay, ei, ey	like **igh** in high	igh	**mein**	mighn
au	like **ow** in now	ow	**auf**	owf
äu, eu	like **oy** in boy	oy	**neu**	noy

Some basic expressions

Yes.	**Ja.**	yar
No.	**Nein.**	nighn
Please.	**Bitte.**	**bit**ter
Thank you.	**Danke.**	**dahng**ker
Thank you very much.	**Vielen Dank.**	**fee**lern dahnk
That's all right.	**Gern geschehen.**	gehrn ger**shay**ern
You're welcome.	**Bitte.**	**bit**ter

Greetings

Good morning.	**Guten Morgen.**	**goo**tern **mor**gern
Good afternoon.	**Guten Tag.**	**goo**tern targ
Good evening.	**Guten Abend.**	**goo**tern **ar**bernt
Good night.	**Gute Nacht.**	**goo**ter nahkht
Good-bye.	**Auf Wiedersehen.**	owf **vee**derrzayern
See you later.	**Bis bald.**	biss bahlt
This is Mr...	**Das ist Herr...**	dahss ist hehr
This is Mrs...	**Das ist Frau...**	dahss ist frow
This is Miss...	**Das ist Fräulein...**	dahss ist **froy**lighn
How do you do?	**Wie geht es Ihnen?**	vee gayt ehss **ee**nern
I'm very pleased to meet you.	**Sehr erfreut.**	zayr ehr**froyt**
How are you?	**Wie geht's?**	vee gayts
Very well, thanks. And you?	**Danke, gut. Und Ihnen?**	**dahng**ker goot. unt **ee**nern
How's it going?	**Wie steht's?**	vee shtayts

Excuse me. (I didn't hear).	**Wie bitte?**	vee **bitt**er
Excuse me. (May I get past?)	**Gestatten Sie?**	ger**shtah**tern zee
That's all right.	**Bitte.**	**bitt**er
I beg your pardon.	**Verzeihung. Wie bitte?**	fehr**tsigh**ung. vee **bitt**er

Questions

Where?	**Wo?**	voa
Where is...?	**Wo ist...?**	voa ist
Where are...?	**Wo sind...?**	voa zint
When?	**Wann?**	vahn
What?	**Was?**	vahss
How?	**Wie?**	vee
How much?	**Wieviel?**	vee**feel**
How many?	**Wieviele?**	vee**fee**ler
Who?	**Wer?**	vayr
Why?	**Warum?**	vah**rum**
Which?	**Welche? (Welcher/Welches)**	**vehl**kher (**vehl**kherr/**vehl**kherss)
What do you call this in German?	**Wie heißt das auf Deutsch?**	vee highst dahss owf doych
What do you call these in German?	**Wie heißen diese auf Deutsch?**	vee **high**ssern **dee**zer owf doych
What does this mean?	**Was bedeutet das?**	vahss ber**doy**tert dahss
Do you speak English?	**Sprechen Sie Englisch?**	**shpreh**khern zee **ehng**lish
I don't speak much German.	**Ich spreche kaum Deutsch.**	ikh **shpreh**kher kowm doych

Could you speak more slowly?	**Könnten Sie bitte langsamer sprechen?**	**kurn**tern zee **bit**ter **lahng**zahmerr **shpreh**khern
Could you repeat that?	**Könnten Sie das bitte wiederholen?**	**kurn**tern zee dahss **bit**ter veederr**hoa**lern
Please write it down.	**Schreiben Sie es bitte auf.**	**shrigh**bern zee ehss **bit**ter owf
Can you translate this for me?	**Könnten Sie mir das übersetzen?**	**kurn**tern zee meer dahss ewberr**zeht**sern
Can you translate this for us?	**Könnten Sie uns das übersetzen?**	**kurn**tern zee uns dahss ewberr**zeht**sern
Please point to the phrase in the book.	**Bitte zeigen Sie mir den Satz im Buch.**	**bit**ter **tsigh**gern zee meer dayn zahts im bookh
Just a minute. I'll see if I can find it in this book.	**Einen Augenblick bitte, ich schaue mal im Buch nach ob ich ihn finde.**	ighnern **ow**gernblik **bit**ter ikh **show**er marl im bookh narkh op ikh een **fin**der
I understand.	**Ich verstehe.**	ikh fehr**shtay**er
I don't understand.	**Ich verstehe nicht.**	ikh fehr**shtay**er nikht
Do you understand?	**Verstehen Sie?**	fehr**shtay**ern zee

Can...

Can I have...?	**Kann ich... haben?**	kahn ikh... **har**bern
Can we have...?	**Können wir... haben?**	**kur**nern veer... **har**bern
Can you show me...?	**Können Sie mir... zeigen?**	**kur**nern zee meer... **tsigh**gern
I can't.	**Leider nicht.**	**ligh**derr nikht
Can you tell me...?	**Können Sie mir sagen...?**	**kur**nern zee meer **zar**gern
Can you help me?	**Können Sie mir helfen?**	**kur**nern zee meer **hehl**fern

Can I help you?	**Kann ich Ihnen helfen?**	kahn ikh **ee**nern **hehl**fern
Can you direct me to...?	**Können Sie mir den Weg zu...zeigen?**	**kur**nern zee meer dayn vayg tsu...**tsigh**gern

Wanting...

I'd like...	**Ich hätte gern...**	ikh **heh**ter gehrn
We'd like...	**Wir hätten gern...**	veer **heh**tern gehrn
What do you want?	**Was wünschen Sie?**	vahss **vewn**shern zee
Give me...	**Geben Sie mir...**	**gay**bern zee meer
Give it to me.	**Geben Sie es mir.**	**gay**bern zee ehss meer
Bring me...	**Bringen Sie mir...**	**bring**ern zee meer
Bring it to me.	**Bringen Sie es mir.**	**bring**ern zee ehss meer
Show me...	**Zeigen Sie mir...**	**tsigh**gern zee meer
Show it to me.	**Zeigen Sie es mir.**	**tsigh**gern zee ehss meer
I'm looking for...	**Ich suche...**	ikh **zoo**kher
I'm hungry.	**Ich bin hungrig.**	ikh bin **hung**rikh
I'm thirsty.	**Ich bin durstig.**	ikh bin **door**stikh
I'm tired.	**Ich bin müde.**	ikh bin **mew**der
I'm lost.	**Ich habe mich verirrt.**	ikh **har**ber mikh **fehreert**
It's important.	**Es ist wichtig.**	ehss ist **vikh**tikh
It's urgent.	**Es ist dringend.**	ehss ist **dring**ernt
Hurry up!	**Beeilen Sie sich bitte.**	ber**igh**lern zee zikh **bit**ter

It is/There is...

It is...	**Es ist...**	ehss ist
Is it...?	**Ist es...?**	ist ehss
It isn't...	**Es ist nicht...**	ehss ist nikht
Here it is.	**Hier ist es.**	heer ist ehss
Here they are.	**Hier sind sie.**	heer zint zee
There it is.	**Dort ist es.**	dort ist ehss
There they are.	**Dort sind sie.**	dort zint zee
There is/are...	**Es gibt...**	ehss gipt
Is there/Are there...?	**Gibt es...?**	gipt ehss
There isn't/aren't...	**Es gibt nicht...**	ehss gipt nikht
There isn't/aren't any.	**Es gibt keinen (keine).**	ehss gipt **kigh**nern (**kigh**ner)

It's...

big/small	**groß/klein**	groass/klighn
quick/slow	**schnell/langsam**	shnehl/**lahng**zahm
early/late	**früh/spät**	frew/shpait
cheap/expensive	**billig/teuer**	**bil**likh/**toy**err
near/far	**nah/weit**	nar/vight
hot/cold	**heiß/kalt**	highss/kahlt
full/empty	**voll/leer**	fol/layr
heavy/light	**schwer/leicht**	shvayr/lighkht
open/shut	**offen/geschlossen**	**of**fern/ger**shlos**sern
right/wrong	**richtig/falsch**	**rikh**tikh/fahlsh
old/new	**alt/neu**	ahlt/noy
old/young	**alt/jung**	ahlt/yung
next/last	**nächste/letzte**	**nehkh**ster/**lehts**ter
beautiful/ugly	**schön/häßlich**	shurn/**hehs**likh

free (vacant)	**frei (leer)**	frigh (layr)
occupied	**besetzt**	ber**zehtst**
good/bad	**gut/schlecht**	goot/shlehkht
better/worse	**besser/schlechter**	**beh**sserr/**shlehkh**terr
here/there	**hier/dort**	heer/dort
now/then	**jetzt/dann**	yehtst/dahn

Quantities

a little/lot	**ein wenig/eine Menge**	ighn **vay**nikh/**igh**ner **mehng**er
much/many	**viel/viele**	feel/**fee**ler
more/less (than)	**mehr/weniger (als)**	mayr/**vay**nigerr (ahlss)
enough/too	**genug/zu (viel)**	ger**noog**/tsoo (feel)
some (any)	**einige**	**igh**niger

A few prepositions and some more useful words

at	**an/bei**	ahn/bigh
on	**an/auf**	ahn/owf
in	**in**	in
to	**zu**	tsoo
from	**von**	fon
inside	**drinnen**	**drin**nern
outside	**draußen**	**drow**ssern
for	**für**	fewr
after	**nach**	nahkh
before	**vor**	foar
with	**mit**	mit
without	**ohne**	**oa**ner

through	**durch**	doorkh
towards	**in Richtung auf**	in **rikh**tung owf
until	**bis**	biss
during	**während**	vairernt
and	**und**	unt
or	**oder**	oaderr
not	**nicht**	nikht
nothing	**nichts**	nikhts
none	**kein**	kighn
very	**sehr**	zayr
too (also)	**auch**	owkh
soon	**bald**	bahlt
perhaps	**vielleicht**	fee**lighkht**

Arrival

You've arrived. Whether you've come by ship or plane, you'll have to go through passport and customs formalities. (For car/border control, see page 146.)

There's certain to be somebody around who speaks English. That's why we're making this a brief section. What you really want is to be off to your hotel in the shortest possible time. And here are the steps to get these formalities out of the way quickly.

Passport control

In these days of the jumbo jet, you may well be waved through passport control with a smile. Otherwise:

Here's my passport.	**Hier ist mein Paß.**	heer ist mighn pahss
I'll be staying...	**Ich werde... bleiben.**	ikh **vayr**der... **bligh**bern
a few days	**ein paar Tage**	ighn parr **tar**ger
a week	**eine Woche**	**igh**ner **vo**kher
two weeks	**zwei Wochen**	tsvigh **vo**khern
a month	**einen Monat**	**igh**nern **moa**nart
I don't know yet.	**Ich weiß noch nicht.**	ikh vighss nokh nikht
I'm here on holiday.	**Ich bin auf Urlaub hier.**	ikh bin owf **oor**lowp heer
I'm here on business.	**Ich bin auf Geschäftsreise hier.**	ikh bin owf ger**shehfts**righzer heer
I'm just passing through.	**Ich bin nur auf der Durchreise.**	ikh bin noor owf derr **doorkh**righzer

If things become difficult:

I'm sorry, I don't understand.	**Es tut mir leid, ich verstehe nicht.**	ehss toot meer light ikh fehr**shtay**er nikht
Is there anyone here who speaks English?	**Spricht hier jemand Englisch?**	shprikht heer **yay**mahnt **ehng**lish

ARRIVAL

Customs

The chart below shows what you can bring in duty-free (visitors from overseas are allowed greater concessions as regards duty-free cigarettes and tobacco).*

	Cigarettes		Cigars		Tobacco (grams)	Spirits (Liquor) (lit.)		Wine (lit.)
Germany	1) 300	or	75	or	400	1½	and	3
	2) 200	or	50	or	250	1	and	2
Austria	200	or	50	or	250	1	and	2
Switzerland	200	or	50	or	250	1	and	2

1) Travellers originating from a country belonging to E.E.C.
2) Travellers originating from a European country outside E.E.C.

German customs may inquire about tea or coffee, since only a limited quantity of either is admitted duty-free.

At almost all major airports in Europe, an honour system for clearing customs has been adopted. Baggage is often not even opened, although spot checks are a possibility. After collecting your baggage, you've a choice: follow the green arrow if you've nothing to declare. Or leave via a doorway marked with a red arrow if you've items to declare (in excess of those allowed).

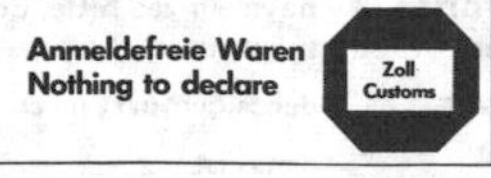

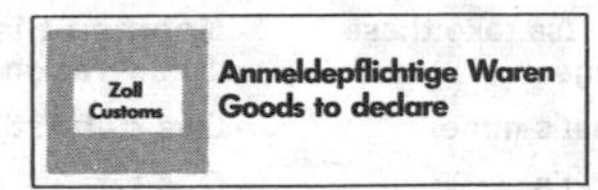

I've nothing to declare.	**Ich habe nichts zu verzollen.**	ikh harber nikhts tsu fehrtsollern
I've...	**Ich habe...**	ikh harber
a carton of cigarettes	**eine Stange Zigaretten**	ighner shtahnger tsiggahrehtern
a bottle of whisky	**eine Flasche Whisky**	ighner flahsher viskee
a bottle of wine	**eine Flasche Wein**	ighner flahsher vighn

*All allowances subject to change without notice and measurements are approximate. Although customs officers hardly ever quibble about the difference between a litre bottle and a quart bottle, they are, of course, entitled to stick to the letter of the law if they choose.

Must I pay on this?	**Muß ich dafür Zoll zahlen?**	muss ikh dahfewr tsol tsarlern
How much?	**Wieviel?**	veefeel
It's for my personal use.	**Das ist für meinen persönlichen Gebrauch.**	dahss ist fewr mighnern pehrzurnlikhern gerbrowkh
It's not new.	**Es ist nicht neu.**	ehss ist nikht noy

Ihren Paß, bitte.	Your passport, please.
Haben Sie etwas zu verzollen?	Do you have anything to declare?
Bitte öffnen Sie diese Tasche.	Please open this bag.
Dies ist zollpflichtig.	You'll have to pay duty on this.
Haben Sie noch mehr Gepäck?	Do you have any more luggage?

Baggage—Porters

The porter may take your bags to customs for you. He'll then wait till they've been cleared. Note the number on his badge.

Porter!	**Gepäckträger!**	gerpehktraigerr
Please take these bags.	**Nehmen Sie bitte diese Taschen.**	naymern zee bitter deezer tahshern
That's mine.	**Das gehört mir.**	dahss gerhurrt meer
That's...	**Das ist...**	dahss ist
my bag	**meine Tasche**	mighner tahsher
my luggage	**mein Gepäck**	mighn gerpehk
my suitcase	**mein Koffer**	mighn kofferr
That...one.	**Dieser...**	deezerr
big/small	**große/kleine**	groasser/klighner
blue/brown	**blaue/braune**	blower/browner
black/plaid	**schwarze/karierte**	shvahrtser/kahreerter
There's one piece missing.	**Ein Stück fehlt.**	ighn shtewk faylt

FOR TIPPING, see inside back-cover

Take these bags...	**Bringen Sie dieses Gepäck...**	**bring**ern zee **dee**zers ger**pehk**
to the bus	**zum Bus**	tsum buss
to the luggage lockers	**zu den Schließfächern**	tsoo dayn **shlees**fehkherrn
to the taxi	**zum Taxi**	tsum **tahk**si
How much is that?	**Wieviel macht das?**	**veefeel** mahkht dahss

Changing money

You'll find a bank at most airports and leading railway stations. If it's closed, don't worry. You'll be able to change money at your hotel.

Full details about money and currency exchange are given on pages 134–136.

Where's the nearest currency exchange?	**Wo ist die nächste Wechselstube?**	voa ist dee **nehkh**ster **vehk**serlshtoober
Can you change these traveller's cheques (checks)?	**Können Sie diese Reiseschecks einlösen?**	**kur**nern zee **dee**zer **righ**zershehks **ighn**lurzern
I want to change some...	**Ich möchte einige... wechseln.**	ikh **murkh**ter **igh**niger... **vehk**serln
dollars/pounds	**Dollar/Pfund**	**dol**lahr/pfunt
Can you change this into...?	**Können Sie das in... umwechseln?**	**kur**nern zee dahss in... **um**vehkserln
German marks	**D-Mark**	day-mahrk
Austrian shillings	**Schilling**	**shil**ling
Swiss francs	**Schweizer Franken**	**shvight**serr **frahn**kern
What's the exchange rate?	**Wie ist der Wechselkurs?**	vee ist derr **vehk**serlkoors

Hotel reservations

Many terminals have a hotel reservation service or tourist information office. You're sure to find someone there who speaks English. There's sometimes a special telephone that connects you to a hotel service or to individual hotels.

FOR NUMBERS, see page 175

Car rental

There are car rental firms at most airports and terminals. It's highly likely that someone there will speak English. But if nobody does, try one of the following:

I'd like a...	**Ich möchte...**	ikh **murkh**ter
car	**einen Wagen**	**igh**nern **var**gern
small car	**einen kleinen Wagen**	**igh**nern **kligh**nern **var**gern
large car	**einen großen Wagen**	**igh**nern **groa**ssern **var**gern
sports car	**einen Sportwagen**	**igh**nern **shport**vargern
I'd like it for...	**Ich möchte ihn für...**	ikh **murkh**ter een fewr
a day/four days	**einen Tag/vier Tage**	**igh**nern targ/feer **tar**ger
a week/two weeks	**eine Woche/zwei Wochen**	**igh**ner **vo**kher/tsvigh **vo**khern
What's the charge per...?	**Wieviel kostet es pro...?**	vee**feel kos**tert ehss proa
day/week	**Tag/Woche**	tark/**vo**kher
Does that include mileage?	**Ist das Kilometer-geld inbegriffen?**	ist dahss killom**may**tergehlt inbergriffern
What's the charge per kilometre?	**Wieviel kostet es pro Kilometer?**	vee**feel kos**tert ehss proa killom**may**terr
Is petrol (gasoline) included?	**Ist das Benzin im Preis inbegriffen?**	ist dahss behn**tseen** im prighss inbergriffern
I want full insurance.	**Ich möchte eine Vollkaskover-sicherung.**	ikh **murkh**ter **igh**ner **fol**kahskoafehrzikherrung
What's the deposit?	**Wieviel muß ich hinterlegen?**	vee**feel** muss ikh hinterr**lay**gern
I've a credit card.	**Ich habe eine Kreditkarte.**	ikh **har**ber **igh**ner kreh**dit**kahrter
Here's my driving licence.	**Hier ist mein Führerschein.**	heer ist mighn **few**rerrshighn

Note: In Germany you can drive on your own licence; but check if an international licence is required for other countries you may visit.

FOR SIGHTSEEING, see page 75

Taxi

All taxis have meters. It's usually best to ask the approximate fare beforehand. For some trips (e.g., airport to town) there may be a fixed rate. This will be posted at the airport.

In principle, the tip is included in the fare in Germany, although it is common to round upwards to the nearest mark.

Where can I get a taxi?	**Wo finde ich ein Taxi?**	voa **fin**der ikh ighn **tahk**si
Please get me a taxi.	**Besorgen Sie mir bitte ein Taxi.**	ber**zor**gern zee meer **bit**ter ighn **tahk**si
What's the fare to...?	**Was kostet es bis...?**	vahss **kos**tert ehss biss
How far is it to...?	**Wie weit ist es bis...?**	vee vight ist ehss biss
Take me to...	**Bringen Sie mich...**	**bring**ern zee mikh
this address	**zu dieser Adresse**	tsu **dee**zerr ah**dreh**sser
the town centre	**in die Stadtmitte**	in dee **shtaht**mitter
the...Hotel	**zum Hotel...**	tsum hoa**tehl**
Turn...at the next corner.	**Biegen Sie an der nächsten Ecke...**	**bee**gern zee ahn derr **nehkh**stern **eh**ker
left/right	**links ab/rechts ab**	lingks ahp/rehkhts ahp
Go straight ahead.	**Geradeaus.**	gerr**ah**derowss
Please stop here.	**Halten Sie hier, bitte.**	**hahl**tern zee heer **bit**ter
I'm in a hurry.	**Ich habe es eilig.**	ikh **har**ber ehss **igh**likh
Could you drive more slowly?	**Bitte fahren Sie langsamer.**	**bit**ter **far**rern zee **lahng**zahmerr
Could you help me carry my bags?	**Könnten Sie mir bitte mit meinem Gepäck helfen?**	**kurn**tern zee meer **bit**ter mit **migh**nerm ger**pehk hehl**fern

ARRIVAL

Hotel—Other accomodation

Early reservation and confirmation are essential in most major tourist centres during the high season. Most towns and arrival points have a tourist information office (Fremdenverkehrsbüro—**frehm**dernfehrkayrsbewroa), and that's the place to go if you're stuck without a room.

Schloßhotel (**shlos**hoatehl)	Over 50 castles and palaces have been converted into hotels in Germany and Austria. They're located in the countryside.
Hotel (hoa**tehl**)	Hotel; simple or fancy, your room will be spotless. You'll doubtless sleep under a quilt filled with duck or goose down. Before you turn in for the night, place your shoes in the corridor outside your room, and next morning you'll find that a kindly elf has cleaned them. *Hotel garni* means that only a room and breakfast are offered.
Rasthaus (**rahst**howss)	Wayside lodge, motel; most are located just off a motorway (turnpike) or principal route.
Gasthaus/Gasthof (**gahst**howss/**gahst**hoaf)	An inn
Pension/Fremdenheim (pehn**zioan**/**frehm**dernhighm)	A boarding-house; offers full or half board. *Zimmer frei* will tell you there's a room to let, sometimes also in a private home.
Jugendherberge (**yoo**gernthehrbehrger)	Youth hostel; there are 700 in Germany alone.
Ferienwohnung (**feh**riernvoanung)	A furnished flat (apartment) found in holiday resorts; you'll probably have to reserve it in advance. Otherwise, contact the local tourist office.

In this section, we're mainly concerned with the smaller and medium-priced hotels and boarding-houses. You'll have no language difficulties in the luxury and first-class hotels where most of the staff speak English.

FOR CAMPING, see page 89

In the next few pages we consider your requirements—step by step—from arrival to departure. You needn't read through all of it. Just turn to the situation that applies.

Checking in—Reception

My name is...	**Ich heiße...**	ikh **high**sser
I've a reservation.	**Ich habe reservieren lassen.**	ikh **har**ber rehzerr**vee**rern **lah**ssern
We've reserved two rooms, a single and a double.	**Wir haben zwei Zimmer reservieren lassen – ein Einzelzimmer und ein Doppelzimmer.**	veer **har**bern tsvigh **tsim**merr rehzerr**vee**rern **lah**ssern—ighn **ighn**tserltsimmerr unt ighn **dop**perltsimmerr
I wrote to you last month.	**Ich habe Ihnen im vergangenen Monat geschrieben.**	ikh **har**ber **ee**nern im fehr**gahng**ernern **moa**naht ger**shree**bern
Here's the confirmation.	**Hier ist die Bestätigung.**	heer ist dee ber**shtai**tigung
I'd like a...	**Ich hätte gern ein...**	ikh **heh**ter gehrn ighn
single room	**Einzelzimmer**	**ighn**tserltsimmerr
double room	**Doppelzimmer**	**dop**perltsimmerr
room with twin beds	**Zimmer mit zwei Betten**	**tsim**merr mit tsvigh **beh**tern
room with a bath	**Zimmer mit Bad**	**tsim**merr mit bart
room with a shower	**Zimmer mit Dusche**	**tsim**merr mit **doo**sher
room with a balcony	**Zimmer mit Balkon**	**tsim**merr mit bahl**koan**
room with a view	**Zimmer mit guter Aussicht**	**tsim**merr mit **goo**terr **ows**sikht
We'd like a room...	**Wir hätten gern ein Zimmer...**	veer **heh**tern gehrn ighn **tsim**merr
in the front	**nach vorn**	nahkh forn
an the back	**nach hinten**	nahkh **hin**tern
facing the sea	**mit Blick aufs Meer**	mit blik owfs mayr
facing the courtyard	**mit Blick auf den Hof**	mit blik owf dayn hoaf
It must be quiet.	**Es muß ruhig sein.**	ehss muss **roo**ikh zighn

Is there...?	**Gibt es...?**	gipt ehss
air conditioning?	**Klimaanlage**	**klee**mahahnlarger
heating	**Heizung**	**high**tsung
a radio in the room	**Radio im Zimmer**	rardio im **tsimm**err
a television in the room	**Fernsehen im Zimmer**	**fehrn**zayern im **tsimm**err
laundry service	**einen Wäschedienst**	**igh**nern **weh**sherdeenst
room service	**Zimmerbedienung**	**tsimm**errberdeenung
hot water	**warmes Wasser**	**vahr**merss **vah**sserr
running water	**fließendes Wasser**	**flee**sserndess **vah**sserr
a private toilet	**eine eigene Toilette**	**igh**ner **igh**gerner toy**leh**ter

How much?

What's the price...?	**Wieviel kostet es...?**	vee**feel kos**tert ehss
per week	**pro Woche**	proa **vo**kher
per night	**pro Nacht**	proa nahkht
for bed and breakfast	**für Übernachtung mit Frühstück**	fewr ewberr**nahkh**tung mit **frew**shtewk
excluding meals	**ohne Mahlzeiten**	**oa**ner **marl**tsightern
for full board	**mit Vollpension**	mit **fol**pehnzioan
for half board	**mit Halbpension**	mit **hahlp**pehnzioan
Does that include...?	**Ist...inbegriffen?**	ist... **in**bergriffern
breakfast	**Frühstück**	**frew**shtewk
meals	**Essen**	**eh**ssern
service	**Bedienung**	ber**dee**nung
Value-Added Tax*	**Mehrwertsteuer**	**mayr**vayrtshtoyerr
Is there any reduction for children?	**Gibt es Ermäßigung für Kinder?**	gipt ehss ehr**mai**ssigung fewr **kin**derr
Do you charge for the baby?	**Berechnen Sie etwas für das Baby?**	ber**rehkh**nern zee **eht**vahss fewr dahss **bay**bee
That's too expensive.	**Das ist zu teuer.**	dahss ist tsu **toy**err
Haven't you anything cheaper?	**Haben Sie nichts Billigeres?**	**har**bern zee nikhts **bil**ligerrers

*Americans note: a type of sales tax

FOR NUMBERS, see page 175

How long?

We'll be staying...	**Wir bleiben...**	veer **bligh**bern
overnight only	**nur eine Nacht**	noor **igh**ner nahkht
a few days	**einige Tage**	**igh**niger **tar**ger
a week (at least)	**(mindestens) eine Woche**	(mindersterns) **igh**ner vokher
I don't know yet.	**Ich weiß noch nicht.**	ikh vighss nokh nikht

Decision

May I see the room?	**Kann ich das Zimmer sehen?**	kahn ikh dahss **tsim**merr zayern
No, I don't like it.	**Nein, es gefällt mir nicht.**	nighn ehss ger**fehlt** meer nikht
It's too...	**Es ist zu...**	ehss ist tsu
cold/hot	**kalt/warm**	kahlt/vahrm
dark/small	**dunkel/klein**	**dung**korl/klighn
noisy	**laut**	lowt
I asked for a room with a bath.	**Ich wollte ein Zimmer mit Bad.**	ikh **vol**ter ighn **tsim**merr mit bart
Do you have anything...?	**Haben Sie etwas...?**	**har**bern zee **eht**vahss
better/bigger	**Besseres/Größeres**	**beh**sserers/**grur**sserrers
cheaper/quieter	**Billigeres/Ruhigeres**	**bil**ligerrers/**roo**igerrers
higher up/lower down	**weiter oben/weiter unten**	**vigh**terr **oa**bern/**vigh**terr **un**tern
Do you have a room with a better view?	**Haben Sie ein Zimmer mit einer besseren Aussicht?**	**har**bern zee ighn **tsim**merr mit **igh**nerr **beh**sserern **ows**sikht
That's fine. I'll take it.	**Das ist gut. Ich nehme es.**	dahss ist goot. ikh **nay**mer ehss

Bills

These are usually paid weekly or upon departure if you stay less than a week. Some hotels offer a reduction for infants and children.

FOR DAYS OF THE WEEK, see page 181

Tipping

A service charge (10–15 %) is normally included in the bill, but you can ask:

Is service included?	**Ist die Bedienung inbegriffen?**	ist dee ber**dee**nung **in**bergriffern

Tipping is moderate in Germany. One or two marks will do for the man who carries your bags to your room. Leave five marks per week for the maid. Tip your waiter and the porter at the time you leave.

Registration

Upon arrival at a hotel or boarding-house you'll be asked to fill in a registration form (*Anmeldungsformular*—**ahn**mehldungsformullarr). It asks your name, home address, passport number and further destination. It's almost certain to carry an English translation. If it doesn't, ask the desk-clerk:

What does this mean?	**Was bedeutet das?**	vahss ber**doy**tert dahss

The desk-clerk will probably ask you for your passport. He may want to keep it for a while. Don't worry. You'll get it back. He may want to ask you the following questions:

Kann ich Ihren Paß sehen?	May I see your passport?
Würden Sie bitte dieses Anmeldeformular ausfüllen?	Would you mind filling in this registration form?
Unterschreiben Sie hier, bitte.	Please sign here.
Wie lange bleiben Sie?	How long will you be staying?

What's my room number?	**Welche Zimmernummer habe ich?**	**vehl**kher **tsim**merrnummerr **har**ber ikh
Will you have our bags sent up?	**Bitte schicken Sie unser Gepäck hinauf.**	**bit**ter **shik**kern zee **un**zerr ger**pehk** hin**nowf**

Service, please

bellboy	**der Hotelpage**	derr hoa**tehl**parzher
maid	**das Zimmermädchen**	dahss **tsim**merrmaitkhern
manager	**der Geschäftsführer**	derr ger**shehfts**fewrerr
room service	**der Hausdiener**	derr **hows**deenerr
switchboard operator	**die Telephonistin**	dee tehlerfonnistin
waiter	**der Kellner**	derr **kehl**nerr
waitress	**die Kellnerin/ Serviererin**	dee **kehl**nerrin/ sehr**vee**rerrin

If you want to address members of the staff, don't say *Herr*, *Frau* or *Fräulein*, but use a general introductory phrase such as:

Excuse me. Could you please...?	**Entschuldigen Sie. Könnten Sie bitte...?**	ehnt**shul**digern zee. **kurn**tern zee **bit**ter

General requirements

Please ask the maid to come up.	**Bitte schicken Sie das Zimmermädchen herauf.**	bitter **shik**kern zee dahss **tsim**merrmaitkhern hehr**owf**
Who is it?	**Wer ist da?**	vayr ist dar
Just a minute.	**Einen Augenblick, bitte.**	**igh**nern owgern**blik** **bit**ter
Come in!	**Herein!**	hehr**ighn**
The door's open.	**Die Tür ist offen.**	dee tewr ist **of**fern
Where is the bath?	**Wo ist das Bad?**	voa ist dahss bart
Where's the plug for the shaver?	**Wo ist die Steckdose für den Rasierapparat?**	voa ist dee **shtehk**doazer fewr dayn rah**zeer**ahpahraht
What's the voltage here?	**Welche Stromspannung haben Sie hier?**	**vehl**kher **shtroam**shpahnung **har**bern zee heer
Can we have breakfast in our room?	**Können wir im Zimmer frühstücken?**	**kur**nern veer im **tsim**merr **frew**shtewkern

HOTEL SERVICE

I'd like to leave this in your safe.	**Ich möchte dies gern in Ihrem Tresor lassen.**	ikh **murkh**ter deess gehrn in **ee**rerm treh**zoar lah**ssern
May I have a/an/some...?	**Kann ich... haben?**	kahn ikh... **har**bern
ashtray	**einen Aschenbecher**	**igh**nern **ah**shernbehkherr
bath towel	**ein Badetuch**	ighn **bar**dertookh
(extra) blanket	**eine (extra) Decke**	**igh**ner (**ek**strar) **deh**ker
envelopes	**Briefumschläge**	**bree**fumshlaiger
(more) hangers	**(noch) einige Kleiderbügel**	(nokh) **igh**niger **kligh**derrbewgerl
ice cubes	**Eisstückchen**	**ighs**shtewkkhern
extra pillow	**ein extra Kopfkissen**	**ighn ek**strar **kopf**kissern
reading-lamp	**eine Leselampe**	**igh**ner **lay**zerlahmper
soap	**Seife**	**zigh**fer
writing-paper	**Schreibpapier**	**shrighp**pahpeer
Where's the...?	**Wo ist...?**	voa ist
barber's	**der Herrenfriseur**	derr **heh**rernfrizurr
bathroom	**das Bad**	dahss bart
beauty parlour	**der Kosmetiksalon**	derr kos**may**tiksahlong
cocktail lounge	**die Bar**	dee barr
dining-room	**der Speisesaal**	derr **shpigh**zerzarl
hairdresser's	**der Damenfriseur**	derr **dar**mernfrizurr
restaurant	**das Restaurant**	dahss rehstor**rahng**
television room	**der Fernsehraum**	derr **fehrn**zayrowm
toilet	**die Toilette**	dee toah**leh**ter

Breakfast

The German breakfast consists of coffee, *Brötchen* (**brurt**khern—crisp buns or rolls, called *Semmeln*—**zeh**merln in Austria and Southern Germany), *Hörnchen* (**hurrn**khern—flaky pastry in the shape of a crescent) and jam.

I'll have a/an/some...	**Ich hätte gern...**	ikh **heh**ter gehrn
bacon and eggs	**Speck und Eier**	shpehk unt **igh**err
eggs	**Eier**	**igh**err
boiled egg	**ein gekochtes Ei**	ighn ger**kokh**terss igh
soft/medium/hard	**weich/wachsweich/hartgekocht**	vighkh/**vahks**vighkh/**hahrt**gerkokht
fried eggs	**Spiegeleier**	**shpee**gerligherr
scrambled eggs	**Rühreier**	**rewr**igherr

fruit juice	**Fruchtsaft**	**frukht**saft
grapefruit	**Pampelmusen**	**pahm**perlmoozern
orange	**Apfelsinen**	ahpferl**zee**nern
ham and eggs	**Schinken und Eier**	**shin**kern unt **igh**err
jam	**Marmelade**	mahrmeh**lar**der
marmalade	**Apfelsinen-marmelade**	ahpferl**zee**nern-mahrmehlarder
omelet	**ein Omelett**	ighn **om**leht
toast	**Toast**	toast
yoghurt	**Joghurt**	**yoa**goort
May I have some...?	**Ich hätte gern...**	ikh **heh**ter gehrn
hot milk/cold milk	**warme Milch/kalte Milch**	**vahr**mer milkh/**kahl**ter milkh
cream/sugar	**Sahne/Zucker**	**zar**ner/**tsuk**kerr
bread/rolls	**Brot/Brötchen**	broat/**brurt**khern
butter	**Butter**	**but**terr
salt/pepper	**Salz/Pfeffer**	zahlts/**pfeh**ferr
coffee/tea	**Kaffee/Tee**	**kah**fay/tay
chocolate	**Kakao**	kah**ka**hoa
lemon/honey	**Zitrone/Honig**	tsi**troa**ner/**hoa**nikh
Could you bring me a...?	**Können Sie mir... bringen?**	**kur**nern zee meer... **bring**ern
plate	**einen Teller**	**igh**nern **teh**lerr
glass/cup	**ein Glas/eine Tasse**	ighn glarss/**igh**ner **tah**sser
knife/fork	**ein Messer/eine Gabel**	ighn **meh**sserr/**igh**ner **gar**berl
spoon	**einen Löffel**	**igh**nern **lur**ferl

Difficulties

The...doesn't work.	**...funktioniert nicht.**	...funktion**neert** nikht
air-conditioner	**die Klimaanlage**	dee **klee**marahnlarger
fan	**der Ventilator**	derr vehntil**lar**toar
heating	**die Heizung**	dee **high**tsung
light	**das Licht**	dahss likht
radio	**das Radio**	dahss **rar**dio
tap	**der Wasserhahn**	derr **vah**sserharn
toilet	**die Toilette**	dee toah**leh**ter
ventilator	**der Lüfter**	derr **lew**fterr
The wash-basin is clogged.	**Das Waschbecken ist verstopft.**	dahss **vahsh**behkern ist fehr**shtopft**

FOR EATING OUT, see pages 38–64

The window is jammed.	**Das Fenster klemmt.**	dahss **fehn**sterr klehmt
The blind is stuck.	**Die Jalousie klemmt.**	dee zhahloo**zee** klehmt
These aren't my shoes.	**Dies sind nicht meine Schuhe.**	deess zint nikht **migh**ner **shoo**er
This isn't my laundry.	**Das ist nicht meine Wäsche.**	dahss ist nikht **migh**ner **veh**sher
There's no hot water.	**Es kommt kein warmes Wasser.**	ehss komt kighn **vahr**mers **vah**sserr
I've lost my watch.	**Ich habe meine Uhr verloren.**	ikh **har**ber **migh**ner oor fehr**loa**rern
I've left my key in my room.	**Ich habe meinen Schlüssel im Zimmer gelassen.**	ikh **har**ber **migh**nern **shlew**sserl im **tsim**merr ger**lah**ssern
The...is broken.	**... ist kaputt.**	... ist kah**put**
bulb	**die Glühbirne**	dee **glew**beerner
lamp	**die Lampe**	dee **lahm**per
plug	**die Steckdose**	dee **shtehk**doazer
shutter	**das Rollo**	dahss **rol**loa
switch	**der Schalter**	derr **shahl**terr
window shade	**die Sonnenblende**	dee **son**nernblehnder
Can you get it repaired?	**Können Sie es reparieren lassen?**	**kur**nern zee ehss rehpah**ree**rern **lah**ssern

Telephone—Mail—Callers

Can you get me Vienna 123456?	**Können Sie mich mit Wien 123456 verbinden?**	**kur**nern zee mikh mit veen 123456 fehr**bin**dern
Did anyone telephone me?	**Hat mich jemand angerufen?**	haht mikh **yay**mahnt **ahn**gerroofern
Do you have stamps?	**Haben Sie Briefmarken?**	**har**bern zee **breef**mahrkern
Would you please mail this for me?	**Könnten Sie das bitte für mich aufgeben?**	**kurn**tern zee dahss **bi**tter fewr mikh **owf**gaybern
Are there any messages for me?	**Hat jemand für mich eine Nachricht hinterlassen?**	haht **yay**mahnt fewr mikh **igh**ner **narkh**rikht hinterr**lah**ssern

FOR POST OFFICE AND TELEPHONE, see pages 137–141

Checking out

May I please have my bill?	**Kann ich bitte die Rechnung haben?**	kahn ikh **bit**ter dee **rehkh**nung **har**bern
I'm leaving early tomorrow. Please have my bill ready.	**Ich reise morgen früh ab. Bereiten Sie bitte meine Rechnung vor.**	ikh **righ**zer **mor**gern frew ahp. ber**right**ern zee **bit**ter **migh**ner **rehkh**nung foar
We'll be checking out around noon.	**Wir fahren gegen Mittag ab.**	veer **far**rern **gay**gern **mit**tark ahp
I must leave at once.	**Ich muß sofort abreisen.**	ikh muss zoa**fort** **ahp**righzern
Is everything included?	**Ist alles inbegriffen?**	ist **ah**lerss **in**bergriffern
You've made a mistake in this bill, I think.	**Ich glaube, Sie haben sich verrechnet.**	ikh **glow**ber zee **har**bern zikh fehr**rehkh**nert
Can you get us a taxi?	**Können Sie uns ein Taxi bestellen?**	**kur**nern zee uns ighn **tah**ksi ber**shteh**lern
When's the next train to Hamburg?	**Wann geht der nächste Zug nach Hamburg?**	vahn gayt derr **naikh**ster tsoog nakh **hahm**boorg
plane/bus	**das Flugzeug/der Bus**	dahss **floog**tsoyg/derr buss
Would you send someone to bring down our baggage?	**Würden Sie bitte unser Gepäck hinunterbringen lassen?**	**vewr**dern zee **bit**ter **un**zerr ger**pehk** hin**un**terrbringern **lah**ssern
We're in a great hurry.	**Wir haben es sehr eilig.**	veer **har**bern ehss zayr **igh**likh
Here's the forwarding address.	**Hier ist meine Nachsendeadresse.**	heer ist **migh**ner **narkh**zehnderahdrehsser
You have my home address.	**Sie haben meine Heimatadresse.**	zee **har**bern **migh**ner **high**mahtahdrehsser
It's been a very enjoyable stay.	**Es war ein sehr angenehmer Aufenthalt.**	ehss varr ighn zayr **ahn**gernaymerr **ow**fehnthahlt
I hope we'll come again sometime.	**Ich hoffe, daß wir mal wiederkommen.**	ikh **hof**fer dahss veer marl **vee**derrkommern

FOR TAXI, see page 27

HOTEL SERVICE

Eating out

There are many types of places where you can eat and drink in Germany, Austria and Switzerland.

Bierhalle
(**beer**hahler)

Beer hall; besides beer served from huge barrels, you'll also be able to order hot dishes, sausages, salads and pretzels. The best-known beer halls are those in Munich which has a giant beer festival *(Oktoberfest)* annually in late September.

Café
(kah**fay**)

Coffee shop; besides coffee, you'll be able to get pastries, snacks and drinks. Often a *Konditorei* (pastry shop) will have a salon for coffee and pastries. A *café* is a *Kaffeehaus* in Austria and sometimes called a *Tea-Room* in Switzerland. There's a small dance floor in a *Tanzcafé*.

Gasthaus
(**gahst**howss)

Inn; usually in the country, it offers home-cooking and a folksy atmosphere. Other words for *Gasthaus* are *Gasthof* and *Beisel* in Austria.

Milchbar
(**milkh**barr)

A bar serving mainly plain and flavoured milk drinks with pastries. Also called a *Milchstübl*.

Raststätte
(**rahst**shtaiter)

Roadside restaurant; also called a *Rasthof* in Austria; it's usually found on a motorway (turnpike). Lodging and service-station facilities are on the premises.

Restaurant
(rehstoa**rahng**)

These are generally found only in urban areas. Menus often cater to foreign visitors as well as offering numerous local specialities.

Schnellimbiß
(**shnehl**limbiss)

Snack bar; the English term is also seen. The principal fare is beer and sausages. A sausage stand *(Würstchenstand)* is often quite similar.

Weinstube
(**vighn**stoober)

A cozy type of restaurant found in wine-producing districts where you can sample new wine with simple hot dishes and snacks. In Austria, it's called a *Heuriger* and is identified by a wreath hanging over the portal.

Lunch (*das Mittagessen*—dahss **mit**tahgehssern) is generally served from 11.30 a.m. until 2 p.m.

Dinner (*das Abendessen*—dahss **ar**berntehssern) is served from 6.30 to 8.30 p.m., in large restaurants to 10 or 11 p.m. After this it's usually a case of cold snacks or hot sausages only.

Eating habits

Most restaurants display a menu *(Speisekarte)* outside. Besides the à la carte menu, they'll usually offer one or more set menus *(Menü* or *Gedeck)*. Value-added tax—a type of sales tax *(Mehrwertsteuer* or *Mwst)*—and a service charge *(Bedienung)* are usually included. The tip is up to you. You may want to leave some small change.

A *Tagesgericht* (**tar**gersgehrikht—the day's special) usually offers you a good meal at a fair price.

Terms on the menu like *Spezialität des Hauses, Nach Art des Hauses* or *Unser Küchenchef empfiehlt* will tell you that these items on the menu are specialities of the house.

Was nehmen Sie?	What would you like?
Ich empfehle Ihnen...	I recommend...
Was trinken Sie?	What would you like to drink?
Möchten Sie...?	Do you want...?
...haben wir nicht.	We haven't got...

Hungry

I'm hungry/I'm thirsty.	**Ich habe Hunger/ Ich habe Durst.**	ikh **har**ber **hun**ger/ikh **har**ber doorst
Can you recommend a good restaurant?	**Können Sie mir ein gutes Restaurant empfehlen?**	**kur**nern zee meer ighn **goo**terss rehstoa**rahng** ehm**pfay**lern
Is there an inexpensive restaurant around here?	**Gibt es in der Nähe ein preiswertes Restaurant?**	gibt ehss in derr **nai**er ighn **prighs**vehrterss rehstoa**rahng**

FOR BREAKFAST, see page 34

If you want to be sure of getting a table in well-known restaurants, it may be better to telephone in advance.

I'd like to reserve a table for 4.	**Ich möchte einen Tisch für 4 Personen reservieren lassen.**	ikh **murkh**ter **ighn**ern tish fewr 4 pehr**zoa**nern rehzehr**vee**rern **lah**ssern
We'll come at 8.	**Wir kommen um 8 Uhr.**	veer **kom**mern oom 8 oor

Asking and ordering

Good evening. I'd like a table for 3.	**Guten Abend. Ich hätte gern einen Tisch für 3 Personen.**	**goo**tern **ar**bernt. ikh **heh**ter gehrn **ighn**ern tish fewr 3 pehr**zoa**nern
Could we have a table...?	**Können wir einen Tisch ... haben?**	**kur**nern veer **ighn**ern tish ... **har**bern
in the corner	**in der Ecke**	in derr **eh**ker
by the window	**am Fenster**	ahm **fehn**sterr
outside	**im Freien**	im **frigh**ern
on the terrace	**auf der Terrasse**	owf derr teh**rah**sser
Where are the toilets?	**Wo ist die Toilette?**	voa ist dee toaah**leh**ter
May I please have the menu?	**Kann ich bitte das Menü haben?**	kahn ikh **bit**ter dahss may**new** **har**bern
What's this?	**Was ist das?**	vahss ist dahss
Do you have...?	**Haben Sie...?**	**har**bern zee...?
a set menu	**ein Tagesmenü**	ighn **tar**gersmaynew
local dishes	**Spezialitäten**	shpaytsiahli**tai**tern
Is service included?	**Ist die Bedienung inbegriffen?**	ist dee ber**dee**nung **in**bergriffern
Could we have (a/an) ..., please?	**Könnten wir bitte ... haben?**	**kurn**tern veer **bit**ter ... **har**bern
ashtray	**einen Aschenbecher**	**ighn**ern **ash**ernbehkherr
(another) chair	**(noch) einen Stuhl**	(nokh) **ighn**ern shtool
glass	**ein Glas**	ighn glarss
knife	**ein Messer**	ighn **meh**sserr
napkin	**eine Serviette**	**ighn**er sehr**vyeh**ter
plate	**einen Teller**	**ighn**ern **teh**lerr
serviette	**eine Serviette**	**ighn**er sehr**vyeh**ter
spoon	**einen Löffel**	**ighn**ern **lur**ferl
toothpick	**einen Zahnstocher**	**ighn**ern **tsarn**shtokherr

FOR COMPLAINTS, see page 55

I'd like a/an/ some...	**Ich hätte gern...**	ikh **heh**ter gehrn
aperitif	**einen Aperitif**	**igh**nern ahpehrit**teef**
appetizer	**eine Vorspeise**	**igh**ner **foar**shpighzer
beer	**ein Bier**	ighn beer
bread	**etwas Brot**	**eht**vahss broat
butter	**etwas Butter**	**eht**vahss **butt**err
cabbage	**Kohl**	koal
cheese	**etwas Käse**	**eht**vass **kai**zer
chips	**Pommes frites**	pom frit
coffee	**einen Kaffee**	**igh**nern **kah**fay
dessert	**einen Nachtisch**	**igh**nern **nahkh**tish
fish	**ein Fischgericht**	ighn **fish**gayrikht
french fries	**Pommes frites**	pom frit
fruit	**etwas Obst**	**eht**vass oapst
game	**Wild**	vilt
ice-cream	**ein Eis/eine Glace** (Switzerland)	ighn ighss/**igh**ner **glah**sser
ketchup	**Tomatenketchup**	toa**mar**ternkehtshap
lemon	**etwas Zitrone**	**eht**vahss tsi**troa**ner
lettuce	**Kopfsalat**	**kopf**zahlart
meat	**Fleisch**	flighsh
milk	**Milch**	milkh
mineral water	**ein Mineralwasser**	ighn minneh**rarl**vahsser
mustard	**etwas Senf**	**eht**vahss zehnf
oil	**etwas Öl**	**eht**vahss url
olive oil	**etwas Olivenöl**	**eht**vahss oa**lee**vernurl
pepper	**etwas Pfeffer**	**eht**vahss **pfeh**ferr
potatoes	**Kartoffeln**	kahr**tof**ferln
poultry	**Geflügel**	geh**flew**gerl
rice	**Reis**	righss
roll	**ein Brötchen**	ighn **brurt**khern
salad	**Salat**	zah**lart**
salt	**etwas Salz**	**eht**vahss zahltss
sandwich	**ein Sandwich**	ighn **sehnd**vitsh
seafood	**Meeresfrüchte**	**may**rersfrewkhter
seasoning	**etwas Würze**	**eht**vahss **vewr**tser
soup	**eine Suppe**	**igh**ner **zup**per
spaghetti	**Spaghetti**	shpah**geh**tee
starter	**eine Vorspeise**	**igh**ner **foar**spighzer
sugar	**etwas Zucker**	**eht**vahss **tsuk**kerr
tea	**einen Tee**	**igh**nern tay
vegetables	**Gemüse**	geh**mew**zer
vinegar	**etwas Essig**	**eht**vahss **eh**ssikh
(iced) water	**(Eis-)Wasser**	(ighss-)**vah**sserr
wine	**(einen) Wein**	(**igh**nern)vighn

What's on the menu?

Our menu is presented according to courses. Under each of the headings you'll find an alphabetical list of dishes that might be offered on a German menu with their English equivalent. You can also show the book to the waiter. If you want some fruit, for instance, show him the appropriate list and let him point at what's available. Use pages 40 and 41 for ordering in general.

Here then is our guide to good eating and drinking. Turn to the section you want.

	Page
Appetizers	43
Soup	44
Fish and seafood	45
Meat	47
Game and fowl	49
Potatoes, rice and noodles	50
Vegetables and salads	50
Cheese	52
Fruit	52
Dessert	53
Beer	56
Wine	57
Other drinks	61
Eating light—Snacks	64

Obviously, you're not going to go through every course. If you've had enough say:

Nothing more, thanks.	**Nichts mehr, danke.**	nikhtss mayr **dahng**ker

One could hardly go away hungry from a German table. Meals are rich and satisfying and are often reminiscent of our homecooking. You'll enjoy the succulent sausages, tender potroasted meats, smoked pork, dark breads, rich gravies and sumptuous desserts.

Appetizers

If you feel like something to whet your appetite, choose carefully, for the German appetizer can be filling.

I'd like an appetizer.	**Ich hätte gern eine Vorspeise.**	ikh **heh**ter gehrn **igh**ner **foar**shpighzer
What do you recommend?	**Was würden Sie empfehlen?**	vahss **vewr**dern zee ehm**pfay**lern

Aal	arl	eel
Aal in Gelee	arl in zher**lay**	jellied eel
Appetithäppchen	apeh**teet**hehpkhern	canapés
Artischocken	ahrti**shok**kern	artichoke
Austern	**ow**sterrn	oysters
Bückling	**bew**kling	bloater, kipper
Fleischpastete	**flighsh**pahstayter	meat loaf
Froschschenkel	**frosh**shehnkerl	frog's legs
Gänseleberpastete	**gehn**zerlayberr-pahstayter	pâté, goose liver purée
Hering	**hay**ring	herring
Hummer	**hum**merr	lobster
Käsehäppchen	**kai**zerhehpkhern	cheese sticks
Kaviar	**kar**viahr	caviar
Krabben	**krah**bern	prawn, shrimp
Krebs	krayps	crayfish
Lachs	lahks	salmon
Langusten	lahng**gus**tern	spiny lobster
Makrelen	mah**kray**lern	mackerel
Muscheln	**mush**erln	mussels
Oliven	oa**lee**vern	olives
Pilze	**pilt**ser	mushrooms
Räucheraal	**roy**kherrarl	smoked eel
Räucherhering	**roy**kherrhayring	smoked herring
Russische Eier	**rus**sisher **igh**err	hard-boiled eggs with mayonnaise
Sardellen	zahr**deh**lern	anchovies
Sardinen	zahr**dee**nern	sardines
Schinken	**shing**kern	ham
roher Schinken	**roa**err **shing**kern	cured ham
gekochter Schinken	geh**kokh**terr **shing**kern	boiled ham
Schnecken	**shneh**kern	snails
Spargelspitzen	**shparr**gerlshpitsern	asparagus tips
Thunfisch	**toon**fish	tunny, tuna
Wurst	voorst	sausage
Wurstplatte	**voorst**plahter	assorted cold cuts

German specialities

Bismarckhering (bismahrkhayring)	soused herring with onions
Frisch geräucherte Gänsebrust auf Toast (frish gehroykherrter gehnzerbrust owf toast)	freshly smoked breast of goose on toast
Hoppel-Poppel (hopperl-popperl)	scrambled eggs with diced sausages or bacon
Königinpastete (kurneeginpahstayter)	puff-pastry shell filled with diced meat and mushrooms
Matjeshering (mahtyehshayring)	salted young herring
Matjesfilet nach Hausfrauenart (mahtyehsfeelay nahkh howsfrowernahrt)	fillets of herring with apples and onions
Hausgemachte Rehpastete (howsgehmakhkter raypahstayter)	home-made venison meatloaf
Schinkenröllchen mit Spargel (shingkernrurlkhern mit shpahrgerl)	rolled ham with asparagus filling
Strammer Max (strahmer mahkss)	highly spiced minced pork served with eggs and onions

Soup and stew

German soup can be hearty fare and particularly welcome on a cold day. *Eintopf* is a stew and will usually be a meal in itself.

I'd like some soup.	**Ich möchte gerne eine Suppe.**	ikh murkhter gehrner ighner zupper

Aalsuppe	arlzupper	eel soup
Bauernsuppe	bowerrnzupper	cabbage and frankfurter soup
Bohnensuppe	boanernzupper	bean soup with bacon
Bouillon	boolyong	clear soup
Erbsensuppe	ehrpsernzupper	pea soup
Fischsuppe	fishzupper	fish soup
Fischbeuschelsuppe	fishboysherlzupper	fish roe and vegetable soup
Fridattensuppe	freedahtternzupper	broth with pancake strips

Frühlingssuppe	**frew**lingszupper	spring vegetable soup
Grießnockerlsuppe	**grees**nokkerrlzupper	semolina-dumpling soup
Gulaschsuppe	**goo**lahshzupper	spiced soup of stewed beef
Hühnerbrühe	**hew**nerrbrewer	chicken broth
Kartoffelsuppe	**kahr**tofferlzupper	potato soup
(Semmel-) Knödelsuppe	(**zeh**merl-)**knur**derlzupper	dumpling soup
Königinsuppe	**kur**niginzupper	with beef, sour cream and almonds
Kraftbrühe mit Ei	**krahft**brewer mit **igh**	beef consommé with raw egg
Leberknödelsuppe	**lay**berrknurdelzupper	liver-dumpling soup
Linsensuppe	**lin**zernzupper	lentil soup
Nudelsuppe	**noo**derlzupper	noodle soup
Ochsenschwanzsuppe	**ok**sernshvahntszupper	oxtail soup
Pichelsteiner Eintopf	**pik**herlshtighnerr **ighn**topf	meat and vegetable stew
Schildkrötensuppe	**shilt**krurternzupper	turtle soup
Serbische Bohnensuppe	**zehr**bisher **boa**nernzupper	spiced bean soup
Tomatensuppe	toa**mar**ternzupper	tomato soup
Zwiebelsuppe	**tsvee**berlzupper	onion soup

Backerbsensuppe (**bahk**ehrpsernzupper) — broth served with small, round croutons

Basler Mehlsuppe (**bars**lerr **mayl**zupper) — flour soup with grated cheese (Swiss)

Kaltschale/Kalte Obstsuppe (**kahlt**sharler/**kahl**ter **oapst**zupper) — fruit soup, served chilled, sometimes containing beer or wine

Labskaus (**larps**kowss) — thick stew of minced and marinated meat with mashed potatoes

Fish and seafood

I'd like some fish.	**Ich hätte gerne Fisch.**	ikh **heh**ter **gehr**ner fish
What kind of seafood do you have?	**Welche Meeresfrüchte haben Sie?**	**vehl**kher **may**rersfrewkhter **har**bern zee

Aal	arl	eel
Austern	**ow**sterrn	oysters
Barsch	barsh	freshwater perch
Brasse/Brachse	**brah**sser/**brahk**ser	bream

Dorsch	dorsh	a variety of codfish
Fischfrikadellen	**fish**frikkahdehlern	fish croquettes
Forelle	fore**h**ler	trout
Flunder	**flun**derr	flounder
Garnelen	gahr**nay**lern	prawns
Hecht	hehkht	pike
Heilbutt	**highl**but	halibut
Hering	**hay**ring	herring
Hummer	**hum**merr	lobster
Jakobsmuscheln	**yar**kopsmusherln	scallops
Kabeljau	**kar**berlyow	cod
Karpfen	**kahr**pfern	carp
Krebs	kraypss	crab
Lachs	lahks	salmon
Languste	lahng**goo**ster	spiny lobster
Makrele	mah**kray**ler	mackerel
Muscheln	**mu**sherln	clams/mussels/ cockles
Neunauge	**noy**nowger	lamprey eel
Rotbarsch	**roat**bahrsh	red sea-bass
Salm	zahlm	salmon
Schellfisch	**shehl**fish	haddock
Scholle	**shol**ler	plaice
Seebarsch	**zay**bahrsh	sea bass
Seebutt	**zay**but	brill
Seezunge	**zay**tsunger	sole
Sprotten	**shprot**tern	sprats
Steinbutt	**shtighn**but	turbot
Stint	shtint	smelt
Stör	shturr	sturgeon
Zander	**tsahn**derr	(giant) pike-perch

Here are some of the ways you may want your fish served:

baked	**gebacken**	geh**bah**kern
boiled in bouillon	**blau**	blow
fried	**gebraten**	geh**brar**tern
deep-fried	**im schwimmenden Fett gebacken**	im **shvim**merndern feht geh**bah**kern
grilled	**gegrillt**	geh**grilt**
marinated	**mariniert**	mahrin**neert**
sautéed (in butter)	**(in Butter) geschwenkt**	(in **but**terr) geh**shvehngkt**
smoked	**geräuchert**	geh**roy**khert
steamed	**gedämpft**	geh**dehmpft**

EATING OUT

Meat

Bear in mind that the Germans most often write in one word what would take us two or more. For example, *Rindszunge* is *Rinds-* (beef) and *-zunge* (tongue) or *Kalbsbrust* is breast of veal. So you may have to look under two entries in the following lists to fully understand what's on the menu.

I'd like some...	**Ich hätte gern...**	ikh **heh**ter gehrn
beef	**Rindfleisch**	**rint**flighsh
lamb	**Lammfleisch**	**lahm**flighsh
pork	**Schweinefleisch**	**shvigh**nerflighsh
veal	**Kalbfleisch**	**kahlp**flighsh

Bauernomelett	bow**er**rnomleht	diced bacon and onion omelet
(deutsches) Beefsteak	(**doy**tsherss) **beef**-stayk	hamburger steak
Beuschel	**boy**sherl	veal lungs, heart, glands with lemon sauce
Bierwurst	**beer**voorst	beer sausage
Blutwurst	**bloot**voorst	black pudding (blood sausage)
Bockwurst	**bok**voorst	large frankfurter
Bratwurst	**brart**voorst	fried sausage
-braten	-brartern	joint, roast
-brust	-brust	breast
Bündnerfleisch	**bewnd**nerrflighsh	cured, dried beef served in paper-thin slices
Eisbein	**ighs**bighn	pickled pig's knuckle
Faschiertes	fah**sheer**terss	minced meat
Filetsteak	fil**lay**stayk	beef steak
Fleischkäse	**flighsh**kaize	type of bologna sausage
Frikadellen	frikah**deh**lern	croquettes
Geschnetzeltes	geh**shneh**tserlterss	chipped veal served in wine sauce
Geselchtes	geh**zehlkh**terss	smoked or salted meat usually pork
Gulasch	**goo**lahsh	gulash; chunks of beef stewed in a rich paprika gravy
Hackbraten	**hahk**brartern	meatloaf
-herz	-hehrtss	heart

EATING OUT

Kasseler Rippenspeer	kahssehlerr rippernshpayr	smoked pork chops
-klößchen	-klursskhern	meatballs
-kotelett	-kotleht	cutlet, chop
Krenfleisch	kraynflighsh	pork, usually brawn, served with shredded vegetables and horseradish
Kutteln	kutterln	tripe
Leber	layberr	liver
Leberkäse	layberrkaizer	type of meatloaf
Nieren	neerern	kidneys
Rippensteak	rippernshtayk	rib steak
Rotwurst	roatvoorst	black pudding (blood sausage)
Rouladen	roolardern	slices of beef or veal filled, rolled and braised (in brown gravy)
Schinken	shingkern	ham
Schlachtplatte	shlahkhtplahter	platter of various sausages and cold meats
Schnitzel	shnitserl	cutlet
Spanferkel	shparnfehrkerl	sucking pig
Speck	shpehk	bacon
Sülze	sewltser	brawn (headcheese)
Wiener Schnitzel	veenerr shnitserl	breaded veal cutlet
-wurst	-voorst	sausage
-zunge	-tsunger	tongue

Here are some hearty dishes you'll certainly want to try:

Bauernschmaus (bowerrnshmowss)	sauerkraut garnished with boiled bacon, smoked pork, sausages, dumplings, potatoes (Austrian)
Berner Platte (behrnerr plahter)	sauerkraut (or green beans) liberally garnished with pork chops, boiled bacon and beef, sausages, tongue and ham (Swiss)
Holsteiner Schnitzel (holshtighnerr shnitserl)	breaded veal cutlet topped with fried egg and usually garnished with pieces of tast, anchovies, mussels, smoked salmon and vegetables
Kohlroulade (koalroolarder)	cabbage leaves stuffed with minced meat
Königsberger Klops (kurnigsbehrgerr klops)	Meatballs in white caper sauce

EATING OUT

How do you like your meat?

baked	**gebacken**	geh**bah**kern
boiled	**gekocht**	geh**kokht**
braised	**geschmort**	geh**shmoart**
broiled	**vom Rost**	fom roast
fried	**(in der Pfanne) gebraten**	(een derr **pfah**ner) geh**brar**tern
grilled	**gegrillt**	geh**grilt**
roasted	**(im Ofen) gebraten**	(eem **oa**fern) geh**brar**tern
stewed	**gedämpft**	geh**dehmpft**
stuffed	**gefüllt**	geh**fewlt**
underdone (rare)	**blutig**	**bloo**tikh
medium	**mittel**	**mit**terl
well-done	**gut durchgebraten**	goot **doorch**gehbrartern

Game and fowl

Back-	**bahk-**	fried
Brat-	**brart-**	roast
-braten	-brartern	joint, roast
Ente	**ehn**ter	duck
Fasan	**fah**zarn	pheasant
Gans	gahnss	goose
Hähnchen	**hain**khern	chicken
Hase	**har**zer	hare
-hendl	-hehndl	chicken
gespickter Hirsch	geh**shpik**terr heersh	larded venison
Huhn	hoon	chicken
Kaninchen	kah**neen**khern	rabbit
Kapaun	kah**pown**	capon
-keule	-koyler	haunch
Masthühnchen	**mahst**hewnkhern	pullet chicken
Rebhuhn	**rehp**hoon	partridge
Reh	ray	venison
-rücken	-rewkern	saddle
Taube	**tow**ber	pigeon, squab
Truthahn	**troot**harn	turkey
Wachtel	**vahkh**terl	quail
Wildschwein	**vilt**shvighn	wild boar

If your meal is prepared *nach Jägerart* (in the hunter's style), it's likely sautéed with mushrooms and root vegetables and served in a wine gravy.

Potatoes, rice and noodles

Brat-	**brart-**	fried
Butterreis	**but**terrighss	buttered rice
Curryreis	**cur**reerighss	curried rice
Geröstel	gehr**urs**terl	hashed-brown potatoes
Kartoffel(n)	kahr**tof**ferl(n)	potato(es)
-bälle	-behler	balls
-brei	-brigh	mashed
-klöße	-klursser	dumplings
-puffer	-pufferr	fritters
-kroketten	-kroakehtern	croquettes
Makkaroni	mahkah**roa**nee	macaroni
Nudeln	**noo**derln	noodles
Pellkartoffeln	**pehl**kahrtofferln	potatoes boiled in their jackets
Petersilienkartoffeln	payterr**zee**liernkahrtofferln	parsleyed potatoes
Pommes frites	pom frit	chips (french fries)
Reis	righss	rice
Röst-	**rurst-**	fried
Rösti	**rursh**tee	hashed-brown potatoes
Salzkartoffeln	**zahlts**kahrtofferln	boiled potatoes
Spätzle	**shpehts**ler	thick noodles
Teigwaren	**tigh**varrern	noodles

EATING OUT

Vegetables, salads

What vegetables do you recommend?	**Welches Gemüse empfehlen Sie?**	**vehl**kherss geh**mew**zer ehm**pfay**lern zee
I'd prefer some salad.	**Ich nehme lieber Salat.**	ikh **nay**mer **lee**berr zah**lart**

Auberginen	oaberr**zhee**nern	aubergines (eggplant)
Blumenkohl	**bloo**mernkoal	cauliflower
Bohnen	**boa**nern	beans
grüne/weiße	**grew**ner/**wigh**sser	green/white
Braunkohl	**brown**koal	broccoli
Champignons	**shahm**pinyong	button mushrooms
Chicorée	sheekoa**ray**	endive (chicory)
Endivien	ehn**dee**viern	chicory (endives)
Erbsen	**ehr**psern	peas
Essiggurken	**eh**ssikhgoorkern	gherkins
Essigkren	**eh**ssikhkrayn	prepared horseradish
Fisolen	fee**soa**lern	french (green) beans

Gemüse	geh**mew**zer	vegetables
gemischtes	geh**mish**terss	mixed vegetables
grüner Salat	**grew**nerr zah**lart**	green salad
Gurken	**goor**kern	cucumber
Häuptlsalat	**hoyptl**zahlart	lettuce salad
Karfiol	kahrfi**oal**	cauliflower
Karotten	kah**rot**tern	carrots
Kohl	koal	cabbage
Kopfsalat	**kopf**zahlart	lettuce salad
Kürbis	**kewr**biss	pumpkin
Lauch	lowkh	leeks
Leipziger Allerlei	**lighp**tseegerr **ah**lerrligh	peas, carrots, asparagus
Mais	mighss	maize (corn)
Meerrettich	**mayr**rehtikh	horseradish
Mohrrüben	**moar**rewbern	carrots
Paradeiser	pahrah**digh**zerr	tomatoes
Pfifferlinge	**pfif**ferrlinger	chanterelle mushrooms
Pilze	**pil**tser	mushrooms
Radieschen	rah**dees**khern	radishes
Rosenkohl	**roa**zernkoal	brussels sprouts
rote Beete/Rüben	**roa**ter **bay**ter/**rew**bern	beetroot
Rotkohl	**roat**koal	red cabbage
Salat	zah**lart**	salad
gemischter	geh**mish**terr	mixed salad
Sauerkraut	**zow**errkrowt	sauerkraut
Schwarzwurzeln	**shvahrts**voortserln	salsify
Sellerie	**zeh**lerree	celery
Spargel	**shparr**gerl	asparagus
Spargelspitzen	**shparr**gerlshpitsern	asparagus tips
Spinat	shpee**nart**	spinach
Tomaten	tom**mar**tern	tomatoes
Weißkohl	**vighs**koal	cabbage
Zwiebeln	**tsvee**berln	onions

Vegetables may be served…

boiled	**gekocht**	geh**kokht**
creamed	**-püree**	**pewray**
diced	**gehackt**	geh**hahkt**
grilled	**gegrillt**	geh**grilt**
stewed	**gedämpft**	geh**dehmpft**

EATING OUT

Cheese

Most of the cheese produced in Germany, Austria and Switzerland is mild. Though there's no cheese course like in neighbouring France, you may see *Käseteller* (**kai**zertehlerr) on the menu. This means you'll get a plate of three or four varieties of cheese, doubtless including the renowned *Emmentaler* (**eh**merntarlerr), which we call simply Swiss cheese. Here are other favourite types of cheese:

mild	Allgäuer Bergkäse (like Swiss cheese), Allgäuer Rahmkäse, Altenburger (made of goat's milk), Appenzeller, Edamer, Greyerzer, Kümmelkäse (made with caraway seeds), Quark, Räucherkäse (smoked cheese), Schichtkäse, Sahnekäse, Tilsiter, Topfen, Weißkäse.
sharp	Handkäse, Harzer Käse, Schabzieger.

Fruit

Do you have (fresh) fruit?	**Haben Sie (frisches) Obst?**	**har**bern zee (**fri**sherss) oapst
I'd like a fruit cocktail.	**Ich hätte gern einen Obstsalat.**	ikh **heh**ter gehrn **igh**nern **oapst**zahlart

Ananas	**ah**nahnahss	pineapple
Apfel	**ah**pferl	apple
Apfelsine	ahpferl**zee**ner	orange
Aprikosen	ahpree**koa**zern	apricots
Banane	bah**nar**ner	banana
Birne	**beer**ner	pear
Blaubeeren	**blow**bayrern	bilberries (blueberries)
Brombeeren	**brom**bayrern	blackberries
Datteln	**dah**terln	dates
Erdbeeren	**ehrt**bayrern	strawberries
Johannisbeeren	yoa**hah**nisbayrern	currants
Feigen	**figh**gern	figs
Haselnüsse	**har**zerlnewsser	hazelnuts
Heidelbeeren	**high**derlbayrern	bilberries (blueberries)
Himbeeren	**him**bayrern	raspberries
Kirschen	**keer**shern	cherries
Kokosnuß	**kok**kosnuss	coconut
Mandarine	mahndah**ree**ner	tangerine
Mandeln	**mahn**derln	almonds
Marillen	mar**ril**lern	apricots
Mirabellen	meerah**beh**lern	a variety of plums

EATING OUT

Melone	may**loaner**	melon (cantaloupe)
Nüsse	**new**sser	nuts
gemischte Nüsse	geh**mish**ter **new**sser	assorted nuts
Pampelmuse	**pahm**perlmoozer	grapefruit
Pfirsich	**pfeer**zikh	peach
Pflaumen	**pflow**mern	plums
Preiselbeeren	**prigh**zerlbayrern	cranberries
Quitte	**kvit**ter	quince
Reineclauden	rainer**kloa**dern	greengages
Rhabarber	rah**bahr**berr	rhubarb
Stachelbeeren	**shtah**kherlbayrern	gooseberries
Trauben	**trow**bern	grapes
Walnüsse	**vahl**newsser	walnuts
Wassermelone	**vah**sserrmayloaner	watermelon
Weintrauben	**vighn**trowbern	grapes
Zuckermelone	**tsuk**kerrmayloaner	honeydew melon
Zwetsch(g)en	**tsveh**tsh(g)ern	plums

Dessert

If you've survived all the courses on the menu, you may want to say:

I'd like a dessert, please.	**Ich hätte gerne eine Nachspeise.**	ikh **heh**ter **geh**rner **igh**ner **nar**khshpighzer
Something light, please.	**Etwas Leichtes, bitte.**	**eht**vahss **lighkh**terss **bit**ter
Just a small portion.	**Nur eine kleine Portion.**	noor **igh**ner **kligh**ner ports**yoan**
Nothing more, thanks.	**Nein danke, nichts mehr.**	nighn **dahng**ker nikhtss mayr

If you aren't sure what to order, ask the waiter:

What do you recommend?	**Was empfehlen Sie?**	vahss ehm**pfay**lern zee

Here are some basic words you'll need to know if you want to order a dessert:

-creme	-kraym	pudding
-eis, -glace	-ighss -glahsser	ice-cream
-kuchen	-kookhern	cake
-pudding	-pudding	pudding
-torte	-torter	layer cake

These flavours of ice-cream are popular throughout Germany:

Erdbeer-	**ehrt**bayr-	strawberry
Karamel-	kahrah**mehl**-	caramel
Mokka-	**mok**kah-	coffee
Schokoladen-	shokkol**lar**dern-	chocolate
Vanille-	vah**nil**ler-	vanilla
Zitronen-	tsi**troa**nern-	lemon

Here are the names of some favourite biscuits (cookies):

Honigkuchen	**hoa**nikhkookhern	honey biscuits
Leckerli	**leh**kerrli	gingersnaps
Makronen	mah**kroa**nern	coconut macaroons
Printen	**prin**tern	honey biscuits
Spekulatius	shpehkoo**lart**siuss	almond biscuits

If you'd like to try something more filling with your coffee, we'd recommend...

Apfelstrudel (**ah**pferlshtrooderl)	paper-thin layers of pastry filled with apple slices, nuts, raisins and ham
Berliner (behr**lee**nerr)	jam doughnut
Bienenstich (**bee**nernshtikh)	honey-almond cake
Cremeschnitte (**kraym**shnitter)	napoleon
Gugelhupf (**goo**gerlhupf)	a moulded cake with a hole in the centre, usually filled with raisins and almonds
Hefekranz (**hay**ferkrahnts)	ring-shaped coffee cake
Kaiserschmarren (**kigh**zerrshmahrern)	shredded pancake with raisins served with syrup (Austrian)
Mohrenkopf (**moa**rernkopf)	chocolate meringue with whipped-cream filling
Palatschinken (pahlaht**shing**kern)	pancakes, usually filled with jam, cheese, sausages or nuts and topped with hot chocolate sauce and nuts
Windbeutel (**vint**boyterl)	cream puff

The bill (check)

I'd like to pay.	**Ich möchte gern zahlen.**	ikh **murkh**ter gehrn **tsar**lern
We'd like to pay separately.	**Wir möchten getrennt bezahlen.**	veer **murkh**tern geh**trehnt** beh**tsar**lern
You made a mistake in this bill, I think.	**Ich glaube, Sie haben sich verrechnet.**	ikh **glow**ber zee **har**bern zikh fer**rehkh**nert
What is this amount for?	**Wofür ist dieser Betrag?**	voa**fewr** ist **dee**zerr beh**trarg**
Is service included?	**Ist die Bedienung inbegriffen?**	ist dee ber**dee**nung **in**bergriffern
Do you accept traveller's cheques?	**Kann ich mit Reiseschecks bezahlen?**	kahn ikh mit **righ**zershehks beh**tsar**lern
Thank you, this is for you.	**Danke, das ist für Sie.**	**dahng**ker dahss ist fewr zee
That was a very good meal.	**Das Essen war sehr gut.**	dahss **eh**ssern varr zayr **goot**
We enjoyed it, thank you.	**Danke, es hat gut geschmeckt.**	**dahng**ker ehss haht goot geh**shmehkt**

BEDIENUNG (NICHT) INBEGRIFFEN

SERVICE (NOT) INCLUDED

Complaints

But perhaps you'll have something to complain about:

That's not what I ordered. I asked for...	**Das habe ich nicht bestellt. Ich wollte...**	dahss **har**ber ikh nikht beh**shtehlt.** ikh **vol**ter
May I change this?	**Können Sie mir dafür bitte etwas anderes bringen?**	**kur**nern zee meer **dar**fewr **bit**ter **eht**vahss **ahn**derrerss **bring**ern
The meat is...	**Das Fleisch ist...**	dahss flighsh ist
overdone	**zu stark gebraten**	tsoo shtarrk geh**brar**tern
underdone (too rare)	**zu roh**	tsoo roa
too tough	**zu zäh**	tsoo tsai

This is too...	**Das ist zu ...**	dahss ist tsoo
bitter/sour salty/sweet	**bitter/sauer salzig/süß**	bitterr/**zow**err **zahl**tsikh/zewss
The food is cold.	**Das Essen ist kalt.**	dahss **eh**ssern ist kahlt
What's taking you so long?	**Weshalb dauert es so lange?**	vehs**hahlp dow**errt ehss zoa **lahng**er
This isn't clean.	**Das ist nicht sauber.**	dahss ist nikht **zow**berr
Where are our drinks?	**Wo bleiben unsere Getränke?**	voa **bligh**bern **un**zerrer geh**trehng**ker
Would you ask the head waiter to come over?	**Würden Sie den Oberkellner zu uns bitten?**	**vewr**dern zee dayn **oa**berrkehlnerr tsoo unss **bit**tern

Drinks

Beer

Needless to say, beer is the national drink. Almost every town with a sizable population has at least one brewery. You'll want to try some of the local brews. However, Dortmund and Bavarian beer are found throughout the country.

I'd like a beer.	**Ich hätte gern ein Bier.**	ikh **heh**ter gehrn ighn beer
I'd like a...of beer.	**Ich hätte gern ... Bier.**	ikh **heh**ter gehrn ... beer
a bottle a glass (1/2 pint) a tall glass (a pint) a mug (a quart)	**eine Flasche ein Glas einen halben Liter eine Maß**	**igh**ner **flah**sher ighn glarss **igh**nern **hahl**bern **lee**terr **igh**ner mars
Waiter! Another beer, please!	**Herr Ober, noch ein Bier, bitte!**	hehr **oa**berr nokh ighn beer **bit**ter

Bier vom Faß (draught or draft beer) is considered to have a better taste and is less expensive, too, than bottled beer.

There are many different types of beer. You'll mainly have to ask for:

a dark beer a light beer	**ein Dunkles ein Helles**	ighn **dung**klerss ighn **heh**lerss

But here are some other types of beer produced in German-speaking countries:

Altbier (**ahlt**beer)	a bitter beer with a high hops content
Bockbier, Doppelbock, Märzen, Starkbier (**bok**beer, **dop**perlbok, **mehrt**sern, **shtahrk**beer)	these are beers with a high alcoholic and malt content
Malzbier (**mahlts**beer)	a dark, sweetish beer with a low alcoholic content but high in calories
Pilsener (**pil**zernerr)	has a particularly strong aroma of hops
Radlermaß (**rard**lerrmarss)	A light beer to which a bit of lemonade is added; in north Germany it's called *Alsterwasser* (**ahl**sterrvahsserr)
Weißbier (**vighs**beer)	a light beer brewed from wheat grain; Berliners love a *Berliner Weiße mit Schuß*—*Weißbier* with a shot of raspberry juice.

Wine

The best wine-producing regions of Germany are those round the Rhine and Moselle rivers—the northernmost wine-producing areas of Europe.

More so than French vintners to the west, German wine producers are at the mercy of the vagaries of the country's climatic conditions. One type of wine can have a quite different character from one year to the next depending upon the weather. Therefore unless you're a German wine expert, you won't know from the wine list how the wine will taste.

For this reason, you'll have to learn to recognize a few basic terms on German labels which will tell you something about how you can likely expect a certain wine to taste. And the Germans are quite precise in labeling wine bottles.

In good years wine may be labeled *naturrein* or *Naturwein* which just means it's been produced under ordinary methods. In a bad year, sugar is sometimes added to increase the alcoholic content. If this is done, *verbessert* (improved) is euphemistically printed on the label.

The time-honoured rule of thumb on wine drinking has it that white wine goes well with fish, fowl and light meats while dark meats call for a red wine. A good rosé or dry sparkling wine goes well with almost anything and can accompany the whole meal. However, most German wine ist white, and less attention is paid to the colour of wine.

There are four other words commonly found on German wine labels which you should know. They indicate the ripeness of the grapes when they were picked—or the degree of dryness or sweetness of the wine.

Spätlese (**spait**layzer)	gathered late after the normal harvesting; dry wine
Auslese (**ows**layzer)	selected gathering of particularly ripe bunches of grapes; slightly dry wine
Beerenauslese (**bay**rernowslayzer)	selected overripe grapes, slightly sweet wine
Trockenbeerenauslese (**trok**kernbayrern-owslayzer)	selected dried or raisin-like grapes; one drop of nectar can be squeezed out of each grape; a sweet or dessert wine is produced.

If none of these words appears on the label, you can assume that the wine results from a normal harvest and will therefore be fairly dry.

Don't miss the opportunity to sample local wine. Much of it doesn't travel well and is therefore rarely exported. The chart on the next page will help you to choose your wine.

In neighbouring German-speaking Switzerland, mostly red wine is produced. Austria's Wachau region along the fabled Danube riverbanks produces white wine while Burgenland to the east of Vienna has red wine.

If you need help in choosing a wine, don't hesitate to ask the waiter. He'll often suggest a bottle of local pride, perhaps a special bottling from the restaurateur's own wine cellar.

Type of wine	Examples	Accompanies
sweet white wine	Rheinpfalz is noted for wine in this category; bottles labeled *Trockenbeerenauslese* also fall into this section.	desserts, especially puddings and cake
dry white wine	The Rheingau region produces extraordinary white wine in good vintage years; Moselle wine can usually be counted on to be very dry; wine labelled *Spätlese* or *Auslese* can go into this category as well as those with the term *naturrein* or *Naturwein*.	cold meat or shellfish, fish, boiled meat, egg dishes, first courses, fowl, veal, dishes served with sauerkraut, sausages
rosé	Sometimes referred to as *Schillerwein*	goes with almost anything but especially cold dishes, eggs, pork, lamb
light-bodied red wine	Most local red wine fits into this category, particularly the wine of Austria's Burgenland, German-speaking Switzerland, the Ahr region (look for the names *Ahrweiler, Neuenahr* and *Walporzheim* on the label) and Baden-Württemberg.	roast chicken, turkey, veal, lamb, beef steak, ham, liver, quail, pheasant, stews, dishes served with gravy
full-bodied red wine	A difficult wine to find but a *Spätburgunder* from the Ahr Valley is a good example.	duck, goose, kidneys, most game, goulash, in short, any strong-flavoured preparations
sparkling wine	German *Sekt* comes into this category; some of it rivals French champagne in quality.	if it's dry, it goes with anything; may be drunk as an aperitif or as the climax to the dinner; goes well with shellfish, nuts and dried fruit; if it's sweet, it'll go nicely with dessert and pastry like *Strudel*

I'd like a... of...	**Ich hätte gerne...**	ikh **heh**ter **gehr**ner
bottle	**eine Flasche**	**igh**ner **flah**sher
carafe	**eine Karaffe**	**igh**ner kah**rah**fer
half bottle	**eine halbe Flasche**	**igh**ner **hahl**ber **flah**sher
litre	**einen Liter**	**igh**nern **lee**terr
1/2-pint glass	**ein Viertel...**	ighn **feer**terl
1/4-pint glass	**ein Achtel...**	ighn **ahkh**terl
I want a bottle of white/red wine.	**Ich möchte eine Flasche Weißwein/ Rotwein.**	ikh **murkh**ter **igh**ner **flah**sher **vighs**vighn/ **roat**vighn

If you enjoyed the wine, you may want to say:

Please bring me another...	**Bitte bringen Sie mir noch...**	**bit**ter **bring**ern zee mir nokh
Where does this wine come from?	**Woher kommt dieser Wein?**	voa**hayr** komt **dee**zerr vighn
What is the name of this wine?	**Wie heißt dieser Wein?**	vee highst **dee**zerr vighn
How old is this wine?	**Wie alt ist dieser Wein?**	vee ahlt ist **dee**zerr vighn

A refreshing highball for the ladies is sparkling wine and orange juice, *Damengedeck* (**dar**merngehdehk) or for the men, *Herrengedeck* (**heh**rerngehdehk), which is sparkling wine and beer.

dry	**trocken**	**trok**kern
full-bodied	**vollmundig**	**vol**mundig
light	**leicht**	lighkht
red	**rot**	roat
rosé	**rosé**	roazay
sweet	**süß**	zewss
very dry	**sehr trocken**	zayr **trok**kern
white	**weiß**	vighss
chilled	**gekühlt**	geh**kewlt**
at room temperature	**in Zimmertemperatur**	in **tsim**merr-tehmpayrahtoor

EATING OUT

Other alcoholic drinks

Don't bother asking for any fancy cocktail or highball except in high-class restaurants.

aperitif	**ein Aperitif**	ighn ahpayritteef
beer	**ein Bier**	ighn beer
Bourbon	**ein Bourbon**	ighn "bourbon"
brandy	**ein Weinbrand**	ighn **vighn**brahnt
cider	**ein Apfelwein**	ighn **ah**pferlvighn
cognac	**ein Kognak**	ighn **kon**yahk
cordial	**ein Likör**	ighn lik**kurr**
gin	**ein Gin**	ighn "gin"
gin-fizz	**ein Gin-fizz**	ighn "gin" fiss
gin and tonic	**ein Gin mit Tonic**	ighn "gin" mit **ton**nik
liqueur	**ein Likör**	ighn lik**kurr**
mulled wine	**ein Glühwein**	ighn **glew**vighn
port	**ein Portwein**	ighn **port**vighn
rum	**ein Rum**	ighn rum
Scotch	**ein Scotch**	ighn "scotch"
sherry	**ein Sherry**	ighn "sherry"
vermouth	**ein Wermut**	ighn **vayr**moot
vodka	**ein Wodka**	ighn **vot**kah
whisky	**ein Whisky**	ighn "whisky"
and soda	**mit Soda**	mit **soa**dah

glass	**ein Glas**	ighn glahss
bottle	**eine Flasche**	**igh**ner **flah**sher
neat (straight)	**pur**	poor
on the rocks	**mit Eis**	mit ighss

You'll certainly want to take the occasion to sip a liqueur or brandy after your meal. The names of same well-known wine-distilled brandies are *Asbach-Uralt, Chantré* and *Dujardin*. Here are some other after-dinner drinks:

Apfelschnaps	**ah**pferlshnahpss	apple brandy
Aprikosenlikör	ahprik**koa**zernlikkurr	apricot liqueur
Birnenschnaps	**beer**nernshnahpss	pear brandy
Bommerlunder	bommerr**lun**derr	caraway-flavoured brandy
Doornkaat	**dorn**kart	German gin, juniper-berry brandy
Eierlikör	**igh**errlikkurr	eggflip, eggnog

Heidelbeergeist	**high**derlbayrgighst	blueberry brandy
Himbeergeist	**him**bayrgighst	raspberry brandy
Himbeerlikör	**him**bayrlikurr	raspberry liqueur
Kirschlikör	**kirsh**likkurr	cherry liqueur
Kirschwasser	**kirsh**vahsserr	cherry brandy
(Doppel)Korn	(**dop**perl)korn	grain-distilled liquor, akin to whisky
Kümmel	**kew**merl	caraway-flavoured liquor
Obstler	**oapst**lerr	fruit brandy
Pflümli(wasser)	**pflewm**li(vahsserr)	plum brandy
Steinhäger	**shtighn**haigerr	juniperberry brandy, akin to gin
Träsch	traish	pear and apple brandy
Weizenkorn	**vight**sernkorn	wheat-distilled liquor, akin to whisky
Zwetschgenwasser	**tsvehtsh**gernvahsserr	plum brandy

I'd like a glass of..., please.	**Ich hätte gern ein Glas...**	ikh **heh**ter gehrn ighn glahss
Are there any local specialities?	**Haben Sie hiesige Spezialitäten?**	**har**bern zee **hee**zigger shpehtsiahli**tai**tern
Please bring me a...	**Bitte bringen Sie mir einen...**	**bi**tter **bring**ern zee mir **igh**nern

ZUM WOHL/PROST!
(tsum voal/proast)

CHEERS!

Other beverages

With coffee captured from the Turks after the siege of 1683, Europe's first café made its debut in Vienna. The *Kaffeehaus* (kah**fay**howss)—of which there are 800 today in the Austrian capital alone—is still an important institution where everyone from students and businessmen to housewives and artists can go to meet friends or associates, play cards, or read newspapers and periodicals. Though initiated in Vienna, the *Kaffeehaus* or *Café* takes on more or less the same importance throughout the rest of Austria as well as in Germany and Switzerland.

The ancient Arab dictum still reigns particularly in Viennese coffee shops: "Coffee must be as black as night, sweet as love and hot as hell." You can ask for anything in Austria from a *Nußschwarzer* (**nus**shvahrtserr) or *Neger* (**nay**gerr)—strong black coffee—to an *Einspänner* (**ighn**shpehnerr)—topped with whipped cream—or a *Melange* (may**lahng**zher)—coffee and hot milk topped with whipped cream. That whipped cream (called either *Schlag* or *Schlagobers*—shlarg, **shlarg**-oaberrs in Austria) is the most important garnish for coffee and many pastries and can even be ordered as a side dish. *Kaffeehäuser* will serve anything from simple pastries to luscious, monumental sweet delicacies, and often snacks. Other types of coffee listed below are pretty much standard throughout German-speaking countries.

I'd like a/an...	**Ich hätte gern...**	ikh **heh**ter gehrn
apple juice	**einen Apfelsaft**	**igh**nern **ahpferlzahft**
(hot) chocolate	**eine (heiße) Schokolade**	**igh**ner (**high**ser) shokkol**ar**der
cup of coffee	**eine Tasse Kaffee**	**igh**ner **tah**sser **kah**fay
coffee	**einen Kaffee**	**igh**nern **kah**fay
with cream	**mit Sahne**	mit **zar**ner
with milk	**einen Milchkaffee**	**igh**nern **milkh**kahfay
black coffee	**einen schwarzen Kaffee**	**igh**nern **shvahrt**sern **kah**fay
caffeine-free	**einen koffeinfreien Kaffee**	**igh**nern koffeh**een**-frighern **kah**fay
espresso coffee	**einen Espresso**	**igh**nern ehs**preh**ssoa
iced coffee	**einen Eiskaffee**	**igh**nern **ighs**kahfay
mokka	**einen Mokka**	**igh**nern **mok**kah
(a glass of) milk	**(ein Glas) Milch**	(ighn) glahss milkh
milkshake	**ein Milchmixgetränk**	ighn **milkh**miksgehtrehnk
mineral water	**ein Mineralwasser**	ighn minneh**rarl**vahsserr
orangeade	**eine Orangeade**	**igh**ner orahng**zhar**der
sodawater	**einen Sprudel**	**igh**nern **shproo**derl
squash (soda pop)	**einen Fruchtsaft**	**igh**nern **frukht**zahft
tea	**einen Tee**	**igh**nern tay
with milk/lemon	**mit Milch/mit Zitrone**	mit milkh/mit tsi**troa**ner
iced tea	**Eistee**	**ighs**tay
peppermint tea	**Pfefferminztee**	pfehferr**mints**tay

Eating light—Snacks

The German *Schnellimbiß* (snack bar) offers a more limited choice of menu than we're used to at home. Since most of the snacks are on display, you won't need to say much more than:

I'll have one of those, please.	**Ich hätte gern eins von diesen.**	ikh **heh**ter gehrn ighns fon **dee**zern
Give me two of these and one of those.	**Geben Sie mir davon zwei und davon eins.**	**gay**bern zee meer **dar**fon tsvigh unt **dar**fon ighns
to the left/to the right	**links/rechts**	links/rehkhts
above/below	**darüber/darunter**	dah**rew**berr/dah**run**terr
Please give me a/an/some...	**Bitte geben Sie mir...**	**bit**ter **gay**bern zee meer
biscuits (Br.)	**Kekse**	**kay**kser
bread	**etwas Brot**	**eht**vahss broat
butter	**etwas Butter**	**eht**vahss **but**terr
cake	**Kuchen**	**koo**khern
candy	**etwas Konfekt**	**eht**vahss kon**fehkt**
chocolate bar	**eine Tafel Schokolade**	**igh**ner **tar**ferl shokkol**lar**der
cookies	**Kekse**	**kay**kser
half a chicken	**ein halbes Hähnchen**	ighn **hahl**berss **hain**khern
ice-cream	**ein Eis**	ighn ighss
pastry	**Gebäck**	geh**behk**
roll	**ein Brötchen**	ighn **brurt**khern
with cheese	**Käsebrötchen**	**kai**zerbrurtkhern
with fish	**Fischbrötchen**	**fish**brurtkhern
with sausage	**Wurstbrötchen**	**voorst**brurtkhern
salad	**Salat**	zah**lart**
sandwich	**ein Sandwich**	ighn **sehnd**vitsh
toast	**etwas Toast**	**eht**vahss toast
waffle	**eine Waffel**	**igh**ner **vah**ferl
How much is that?	**Was macht das?**	vahss mahkht dahss

Travelling around

Plane

Very brief—because at any airport or airline office you're sure to find someone who speaks English. But here are a few useful expressions you may want to know:

Is there a flight to Vienna?	**Gibt es einen Flug nach Wien?**	gipt ehss **igh**nern floog nahkh veen
Is it a nonstop flight?	**Ist es ein Direktflug?**	ist ehss ighn dee**rehkt**flug
When's the next plane to Hamburg?	**Wann geht die nächste Maschine nach Hamburg?**	vahn gayt dee **nehkh**ster mah**shee**ner nahkh **hahm**boorg
Do I have to change planes?	**Muß ich umsteigen?**	muss ikh **um**shtighgern
Can I make a connection to Cologne?	**Kann ich einen Anschlußflug nach Köln buchen?**	kahn ikh **igh**nern ahnshlusfloog nahkh kurln **boo**khern
I'd like a ticket to Zurich.	**Ich möchte einen Flug nach Zürich.**	ikh **murkh**ter **igh**nern floog nahkh **tsew**rikh
What's the fare to Berlin?	**Was kostet ein Flug nach Berlin?**	vahss **kos**tert ighn floog nahkh behr**leen**
single (one-way)	**einfacher Flug**	**ighn**fahkherr floog
return (roundtrip)	**Rückflug**	**rewk**floog
What time does the plane take off?	**Wann startet die Maschine?**	vahn **shtahr**tert dee mah**shee**ner
What time do I have to check in?	**Wann muß ich mich melden?**	vahn muss ikh mikh **mehl**dern
What's the flight number?	**Welche Flugnummer ist es?**	**vehl**kher **floog**nummerr ist ehss
What time do we arrive?	**Wann landen wir?**	vahn **lahn**dern veer

ANKUNFT ARRIVAL	**ABFLUG** DEPARTURE

Train

If you're worried about railway tickets or time-tables, go to a travel agency where they speak English or see the desk-clerk at your hotel.

Travel on the main railway lines is generally fast, and the trains run on time. First-class coaches are comfortable; second-class, more than adequate.

To reach out-of-the-way places, you'll find frequent bus services available including the *Kraftpost* or *Postauto*.

Types of trains

TEE (tay ay ay)	Trans-Europ-Express: a luxury international service for which you pay a supplement. First class only, advance reservation required.
Expreß (ehks**prehss**)	A long-distance train, usually coming from or going abroad, stopping only at principal stations (Austria, Switzerland)
Fernschnellzug (**fehrn**shnehltsoog)	Equivalent of the *Expreß* train (Germany).
Schnellzug (**shnehl**tsoog)	Long-distance train making a few more stops than an *Expreß* train (Austria, Switzerland)
D-Zug (**day**-tsoog)	Equivalent of the *Schnellzug* (Germany)
Städteschnellzug (**shteh**tershnehltsoog)	Long-distance train connecting principal cities and stopping only there (Switzerland)
Eilzug (**ighl**tsoog)	Medium-distance train, not stopping at small stations
Personenzug (pehr**zoa**nerntsoog)	Local train, stopping at all stations
Triebwagen (**treep**vargern)	Small diesel coach used for short runs
Schienenbus (**shee**nernbuss)	Equivalent of the *Triebwagen* (Germany)
Triebwagenschnellzug (**treep**vargernshnehltsoog)	Fast diesel used on long-distance runs (Austria)

Here are a few more useful terms:

Schlafwagen (**shlarf**vargern)	Sleeping-car with individual compartments (single, double, tourist) and toilet or lavatory facilities.
Liegewagen (**lee**gervargern)	A coach containing berths with blankets and pillows
Speisewagen (**shpigh**zervargern)	Dining-car
Gepäckwagen (ger**pehk**vargern)	Guard's van (baggage car) with only registered luggage permitted

To the railway station

Where's the railway station?	**Wo ist der Bahnhof?**	voa ist derr **barn**hoaf
Taxi, please!	**Taxi bitte!**	**tahk**si **bit**ter
Take me to the railway station.	**Fahren Sie mich zum Bahnhof.**	**far**rern zee mikh tsum **barn**hoaf
What's the fare?	**Wieviel macht es?**	vee**feel** mahkht ehss

EINGANG	ENTRANCE
AUSGANG	EXIT
ZU DEN BAHNSTEIGEN	TO THE PLATFORMS

Where's the...?

Where is/are the...?	**Wo ist/sind...?**	voa ist/zint
barber's	**der Herrenfriseur**	derr **heh**rernfrizurr
booking office	**die Platzreservierung**	dee **plahts**rehzerrveerung
buffet	**das Buffet**	dahss bew**fay**
currency-exchange office	**die Wechselstube**	dee **wehk**serlshtoober
information office	**die Auskunft**	dee **ows**kunft
restaurant	**das Restaurant**	dahss rehsto**rahng**
left-luggage office (baggage check)	**die Gepäckaufbewahrung**	dee ger**pehk**owfbervarrung
lost-property (lost and found) office	**das Fundbüro**	dahss **funt**bewroa

FOR TAXI, see page 27

luggage lockers	**die Schließfächer**	dee **shlees**fehkherr
news-stand	**der Zeitungsstand**	derr **tsigh**tungsshtahnt
platform 7	**Bahnsteig 7**	**barn**shtighg 7
reservations office	**die Platz-reservierung**	dee **plahts**rehzerrveerung
ticket office	**der Fahrkarten-schalter**	derr **farr**kahrternshahlterr
waiting-room	**der Wartesaal**	derr **vahr**terzarl
Where are the toilets?	**Wo sind die Toiletten?**	voa zint dee toah**leh**tern

Inquiries

When is the...train to Kiel?	**Wann geht der... Zug nach Kiel?**	vahn gayt derr... tsoog nahkh keel
first/last/next	**erste/letzte/nächste**	**ehr**ster/**lehts**ter/**neh**[illegible]ster
What time does the train for Karlsruhe leave?	**Wann fährt der Zug nach Karlsruhe?**	vahn fairt derr tsoog nahkh **karrls**rooer
What's the fare to Basle?	**Was kostet die Fahrt nach Basel?**	vahss **kos**tert dee farrt nahkh **bar**zerl
Is it a through train?	**Ist es ein durch-gehender Zug?**	ist ehss ighn **doorkh**gayernderr tsoog
What time does the train arrive at Münster?	**Wann kommt der Zug in Münster an?**	vahn komt derr tsoog in **mewn**sterr ahn
Is there a dining-car on the train?	**Hat der Zug einen Speisewagen?**	haht derr tsoog **igh**nern **shpigh**zervargern
Is there a sleeping-car on the train?	**Hat der Zug einen Schlafwagen?**	haht derr tsoog **igh**nern **shlarf**vargern
Does the train stop at Ingolstadt?	**Hält der Zug in Ingolstadt?**	hehlt derr tsoog in **in**golshtaht
What platform does the train for Bonn leave from?	**Auf welchem Gleis fährt der Zug nach Bonn ab?**	owf **vehl**kherm glighss fairt derr tsoog nahkh bon ahp
What platform does the train from Hamburg arrive at?	**Auf welchem Gleis kommt der Zug aus Hamburg an?**	owf **vehl**kherm glighss komt derr tsoog owss **ham**boorg ahn
I'd like to buy a time-table.	**Ich hätte gerne einen Fahrplan.**	ikh **heh**ter gehrn **igh**nern **farr**plarn

TRAVELLING AROUND

Es ist ein durchgehender Zug.	It's a through train.
Sie müssen in ... umsteigen.	You have to change at...
Steigen Sie in Heidelberg in einen Personenzug um.	Change at Heidelberg and get a local train.
Bahnsteig 7 ist...	Platform 7 is...
dort drüben/oben links/rechts	over there/upstairs on the left/on the right
Es gibt einen Zug nach Bonn um...	There's a train to Bonn at...
Ihr Zug fährt auf Bahnsteig ... ab.	Your train will leave from platform...
Der Zug hat... Minuten Verspätung.	There'll be a delay of... minutes.

Tickets

I want a ticket to Stuttgart.	**Ich möchte eine Fahrkarte nach Stuttgart.**	ikh **murkh**ter **igh**ner **farr**kahrter nahkh **shtut**gahrt
single (one-way)	**eine einfache Fahrkarte**	**igh**ner **ighn**fahkher **farr**kahrter
return (roundtrip)	**eine Rückfahrkarte**	**igh**ner **rewk**farrkahrter
first class	**erste Klasse**	**ehr**ster **klah**sser
second class	**zweite Klasse**	**tsvigh**ter **klah**sser
Isn't it half price for the boy/girl?	**Kann der Junge/das Mädchen zum halben Preis fahren?**	kahn derr **yun**ger/dahss **mait**khern tsoom **hahl**bern prighss **far**rern
He's/She's 13.	**Er/Sie ist 13.**	ehr/zee ist 13

Erste oder zweite Klasse?	First or second class?
Einfache oder Rückfahrtkarte?	Single or return (one-way or roundtrip)?
Wie alt ist er/sie?	How old is he/she?

TRAVELLING AROUND

All aboard...

Is this the right platform for the train to Vienna?	**Ist das der richtige Bahnsteig für den Zug nach Wien?**	ist dahss derr **rikh**tigger **barn**shtighg fewr dayn tsoog nahkh veen
Is this the right train to Graz?	**Ist das der Zug nach Graz?**	ist dahss derr tsoog nahkh grarts
Excuse me. May I get by?	**Verzeihung. Darf ich bitte durchgehen?**	fehr**tsigh**ung. dahrf ikh **bi**tter **doorkh**gayern
Is this seat taken?	**Ist dieser Platz besetzt?**	ist **dee**zerr plahts ber**zehtst**
I think that's my seat.	**Ich glaube, das ist mein Platz.**	ikh **glow**ber dahss ist mighn plahts
Would you let me know before we get to Bamberg?	**Könnten Sie mir Bescheid geben, wenn wir in Bamberg ankommen?**	**kurn**tern zee meer ber**shight gay**bern vehn veer in **bahm**behrg **ahn**kommern
What station is this?	**Wie heißt dieser Ort?**	vee highst **dee**zerr ort
How long does the train stop here?	**Wie lange hält der Zug hier?**	vee **lahng**er hehlt derr tsoog heer
When do we get to Cologne?	**Wann kommen wir in Köln an?**	vahn **kom**mern veer in kurln ahn

Sometime on the journey the ticket-collector (*der Schaffner*—derr **shahf**nerr) will come around and say: *Fahrkarten, bitte* (Tickets, please)!

Eating

If you want a full meal in the dining-car, you may have to get a ticket from the attendant who'll come to your compartment. There are usually two sittings for lunch and dinner.

You can get snacks and drinks in the buffet-car and in the dining-car when it isn't being used for main meals. On some trains an attendant comes around with a cart with snacks, tea, coffee and soft drinks. At the larger stations an attendant with a refreshment wagon walks alongside the train and takes orders through the window.

First/Second call for dinner.	**Erster/Zweiter Aufruf zum Essen.**	ehrsterr/**tsvigh**terr owfroof tsum **eh**ssern
Where's the dining-car?	**Wo ist der Speisewagen?**	voa ist derr **shpigh**zer-vargern

RAUCHEN VERBOTEN
NO SMOKING

Sleeping

Are there any free compartments in the sleeping-car?	**Sind noch Abteile im Schlafwagen frei?**	zint nokh ahp**tigh**ler im **shlarf**vargern frigh
Where's the sleeping-car?	**Wo ist der Schlafwagen?**	voa ist derr **shlarf**vargern
Where's my berth?	**Wo ist mein Bett?**	voa ist mighn beht
Compartments 18 and 19 please.	**Abteile 18 und 19, bitte.**	ahp**tigh**ler 18 unt 19 **bit**ter
I'd like a lower berth.	**Ich möchte eine untere Liege.**	ikh **murkh**ter **igh**ner **un**terrer **lee**ger
Would you make up our berths?	**Würden Sie unsere Betten machen?**	**vewr**dern zee **un**zerrer **beh**tern **mah**khern
Would you call me at 7 o'clock?	**Würden Sie mich um 7 Uhr wecken?**	**vewr**dern zee mikh um 7 oor **veh**kern
Would you bring me coffee in the morning?	**Würden Sie mir bitte in der Frühe Kaffee bringen?**	**vewr**dern zee meer **bit**ter in der **frew**er **kah**fay **brin**gern

Baggage and porters

Porter!	**Gepäckträger!**	ger**pehk**traigerr
Can you help me with my bags?	**Können Sie mir mit meinem Gepäck helfen?**	**kur**nern zee meer mit **migh**nerm ger**pehk** **hehl**fern

Note: If you want to put your luggage in the guard's van (baggage car), be sure to have it insured.

Can I insure these bags?	**Kann ich dieses Gepäck versichern?**	kahn ikh **dee**zers ger**pehk** fehr**zee**kherrn

FOR PORTERS, see also page 24

Lost!

We hope you'll have no need for the following phrases on your trip... but just in case:

Where's the lost-property (lost-and-found) office?	**Wo ist das Fundbüro?**	voa ist dahss **funt**bewroa
I've lost...	**Ich habe... verloren.**	ikh **harber**...fehr**loarern**
this morning	**heute morgen**	**hoy**ter **morgern**
yesterday	**gestern**	**geh**sterrn
I lost it in...	**Ich habe es in... verloren.**	ikh **harber** ehss in... fehr**loarern**
It's very valuable.	**Es ist sehr wertvoll.**	ehss ist zayr **vayrtfol**

Underground (subway)

The *U-Bahn* (**oo**-barn) in Hamburg, Berlin, Frankfurt and Munich corresponds to the London underground or the New York subway. Lines extend from the centre of the city to the suburbs. A map showing the various lines and stations is displayed outside every station. Pocket maps can be obtained from news-stands and travel agents. Some *U-Bahnen* are still under construction.

The fare is always the same, irrespective of the distance you travel. If you intend to use the *U-Bahn* regularly, get a book of tickets (*ein Fahrscheinheft*—ighn **farr**shighnhehft). This will mean a small saving on fares.

The *U-Bahn* is closed from 1 to 5 a.m.

Where's the nearest underground station?	**Wo ist die nächste U-Bahnstation?**	voa ist dee **nehkh**ster **oo**-barnshtahtsioan
Does this train go to...?	**Fährt dieser Zug nach...?**	fairt **dee**zerr tsoog nahkh
Where do I change for...?	**Wo muß ich nach... umsteigen?**	voa muss ikh nahkh... **um**shtighgern
Is the next station...?	**Ist die nächste Station...?**	ist dee **nehkh**ster shtahts**ioan**

TRAVELLING AROUND

Bus—Tram (streetcar)

In many buses and trams, you pay as you enter. In cities you'll often find automatic ticket dispensers at each stop enabling you to buy your ticket in advance. In some rural buses, you may find the driver also acting as conductor. In big cities you can buy a booklet of tickets *(ein Fahrscheinheft)* for regular journeys.

If the bus carries the sign *Besetzt*, it means that it is full.

I'd like a booklet of tickets.	**Ich möchte ein Fahrscheinheft.**	ikh **murkh**ter ighn **farr**shighnhehft
Where can I get a bus into town?	**Wo hält der Bus, der ins Stadtzentrum fährt?**	voa hehlt derr buss derr ins **shtaht**-tsehntrum fairt
What bus do I take for...?	**Welchen Bus muß ich nach... nehmen?**	**vehl**khern buss muss ikh nahkh... **nay**mern
Where's the...?	**Wo ist...?**	voa ist
bus stop	**die Bushaltestelle**	dee **buss**hahltershtehler
terminus	**die Endstation**	dee **ehnt**shtahtsioan
When is the...bus to Sankt Pauli?	**Wann fährt der... Bus nach Sankt Pauli?**	vahn fairt derr...buss nahkh sahnkt **pow**lee
first / last / next	**erste/letzte/nächste**	**ehr**ster / **lehts**ter / **nehkh**ster
How often do the buses to the airport run?	**Wie oft fahren die Busse zum Flughafen?**	vee oft **far**rern dee busser tsum **floog**harfern
How much is the fare to...?	**Was kostet es nach...?**	vahss **kos**tert ehss nahkh
Do I have to change buses?	**Muß ich umsteigen?**	muss ikh **um**shtighgern
How long does the journey take ?	**Wie lange dauert die Fahrt?**	vee **lahng**er **dow**errt dee farrt

BUSHALTESTELLE	REGULAR BUS STOP
BEDARFSHALTESTELLE	STOPS ON REQUEST

Will you tell me when to get off?	**Können Sie mir bitte sagen, wann ich aussteigen muß?**	**kur**nern zee meer **bit**ter **zar**gern vahn ikh **ows**shtighgern muss
Please let me off at the next stop.	**Lassen Sie mich bitte an der nächsten Haltestelle aussteigen.**	**lah**ssern zee mikh **bit**ter ahn derr **nehkh**stern **hahl**ter-shtehler **ows**shtighgern

Boats

River boats ply up and down the Rhine and Mosel rivers. A boat trip on the Bonn-Rüdesheim stretch of the Rhine, with its medieval castles and steep vineyards, is well worthwhile.

There's also a river-boat connection from Basle, Switzerland, all the way down to Rotterdam in the Netherlands.

There's regular boat service on the River Danube with some steamers offering cabins for overnight trips. The line begins at Passau, West Germany, continues through the wine-producing region of the Wachau and ends in Vienna. But you can follow the Danube to the east from Vienna via Budapest, for instance.

Other modes of transportation

You may also want to try one of these to get around:

bicycle	**das Fahrrad**	dahss **far**rart
boat	**das Boot**	dahss boat
motorboat	**das Motorboot**	dahss **moa**torboat
rowing-boat	**das Ruderboot**	dahss **roo**derrboat
sailing-boat	**das Segelboot**	dahss **zay**gerlboat
helicopter	**der Hubschrauber**	derr **hoop**shrowberr
hitch-hiking	**trampen**	**trahm**pern
horseback riding	**reiten**	**righ**tern
hovercraft	**das Luftkissenboot**	dahss **luft**kissernboat
moped (motor-bike)	**das Motorrad**	dahss **moa**torrart
motorcycle	**das Moped**	dahss **moa**peht

And if you're really stuck, go...

walking	**zu Fuß gehen**	tsu fooss **gay**ern

TRAVELLING AROUND

Around and about—Sightseeing

Here we're more concerned with the cultural aspect of life than with entertainment and, for the moment, with towns rather than the countryside. If you want a guide book, ask...

Can you recommend a good guide book for...?	**Können Sie einen guten Reiseführer über ... empfehlen?**	**kur**nern zee **igh**nern **goo**tern **righ**zerfewrerr **ew**berr ... ehm**pfay**lern
Is there a tourist office?	**Gibt es ein Fremdenverkehrsbüro?**	gipt ehss ighn **frehm**dernfehrkayrsbewroa
Where's the tourist office?	**Wo ist das Fremdenverkehrsbüro?**	voa ist dahss **frehm**dernfehrkayrsbewroa
What are the main points of interest?	**Was sind die Hauptsehenswürdigkeiten?**	vahss zint dee **howpt**zayernsvewrdikhkightern
We're here for...	**Wir sind für ... hier.**	veer zint fewr ... heer
a few hours	**ein paar Stunden**	ighn parr **shtun**dern
a day	**einen Tag**	**igh**nern targ
three days	**drei Tage**	drigh **tar**ger
a week	**eine Woche**	**igh**ner **vo**kher
Can you recommend a sightseeing tour?	**Können Sie eine Stadtrundfahrt empfehlen?**	**kur**nern zee **igh**ner **shtaht**runtfarrt ehm**pfay**lern
Where does the bus start from?	**Wo fährt der Bus ab?**	voa fairt derr buss ahp
Will it pick us up at the hotel?	**Holt er uns im Hotel ab?**	hoalt ehr uns im ho**tehl** ahp
How much does the tour cost?	**Was kostet die Rundfahrt?**	vahss **kos**tert dee **runt**farrt
What time does the tour start?	**Wann beginnt die Rundfahrt?**	vahn ber**gint** dee **runt**farrt
What bus/What tram (streetcar) do we take?	**Welchen Bus/Welche Straßenbahn müssen wir nehmen?**	**vehl**khern buss/**vehl**kher **shtrar**ssernbarn **mew**ssern veer **nay**mern
We'd like to rent a car for the day.	**Wir möchten gern für heute einen Wagen mieten.**	veer **murkh**tern gehrn fewr **hoy**ter **igh**nern **var**gern **mee**tern

FOR TIME OF DAY, see page 178

Is there an English-speaking guide?	**Gibt es einen englischsprechenden Fremdenführer?**	gipts ehss **igh**nern **ehng**lishshprehkherndern **frehm**dernfewrerr
Where is/Where are the...?	**Wo ist/Wo sind...?**	voa ist/voa zint
abbey	**das Kloster**	dahss **kloa**sterr
amusement park	**der Vergnügungspark**	derr fehr**gnew**gungspahrk
aquarium	**das Aquarium**	dahss ah**kvar**rium
artists' quarter	**das Künstlerviertel**	dahss **kewn**stlerrfeerterl
botanical gardens	**der Botanische Garten**	derr bot**tar**nisher **gahr**tern
building	**das Gebäude**	dahss ger**boy**der
business district	**das Geschäftsviertel**	dahss ger**shehfts**feertel
castle	**das Schloß/die Burg**	dahss shloss/dee boorg
catacombs	**die Katakomben**	dee kahtah**kom**bern
cathedral	**die Kathedrale/der Dom**	dee kahteh**drar**ler/derr doam
cave	**die Höhle**	dee **hur**ler
cemetery	**der Friedhof**	derr **freet**hoaf
circus	**der Zirkus**	derr **tseer**kuss
city centre	**die Stadtmitte**	dee **shtaht**mitter
city hall	**das Rathaus**	dahss **rar**thowss
city walls	**die Stadtmauern**	dee **shtaht**mowerr
church	**die Kirche**	dee **keer**kher
concert hall	**die Konzerthalle**	dee kon**tsehrt**hahler
convent	**das Nonnenkloster**	dahss **non**nernkloasterr
convention hall	**die Kongreßhalle**	dee kon**grehs**hahler
court house	**das Gericht**	dahss ger**rikht**
docks	**die Hafenanlagen**	dee **har**fernahnlargern
downtown area	**die Innenstadt**	dee **in**nernshtaht
exhibition	**die Ausstellung**	dee **ows**shtehlung
factory	**die Fabrik**	dee fah**brik**
fortress	**die Festung**	dee **feh**stung
fountain	**der Brunnen/Springbrunnen**	derr **brun**nern/**shpring**brunnern
gallery	**die Galerie**	dee gahleh**ree**
gardens	**die Grünanlagen**	dee **grewn**ahnlargern
government building	**das Regierungsgebäude**	dahss reh**gee**rungsgerboyder
harbour	**der Hafen**	derr **har**fern
lake	**der See**	derr zay
library	**die Bibliothek**	dee biblioa**tayk**
market	**der Markt**	derr mahrkt
memorial	**das Denkmal**	dahss **dehngk**marl
monastery	**das Kloster**	dahss **kloa**sterr
monument	**das Denkmal**	dahss **dehngk**marl

FOR ASKING THE WAY, see also page 144

museum	**das Museum**	dahss muz**ay**um
observatory	**das Observatorium**	dahss opzehrvah**toa**rium
old city	**die Altstadt**	dee **ahlt**shtaht
opera house	**das Opernhaus**	dahss **oa**perrnhowss
palace	**der Palast/das Schloß**	derr pah**lahst**/dahss shloss
park	**der Park**	derr pahrk
parliament building	**das Parlaments-gebäude**	dahss pahrlah**mehnts**-gerboyder
river	**der Fluß**	derr fluss
ruins	**die Ruinen**	dee ru**ee**nern
shopping centre	**das Einkaufszentrum**	dahss **ighn**kowfstsehntrum
stadium	**das Stadion**	dahss **shtar**dion
statue	**die Statue**	dee **shtar**tuer
stock exchange	**die Börse**	dee **burr**zer
television studio	**das Fernsehstudio**	dahss **fehrn**zayshtoodio
tomb	**die Gruft**	dee gruft
tower	**der Turm**	derr toorm
university	**die Universität**	dee unnivehrzi**tayt**
zoo	**der Zoo**	derr tsoa

Admission

Is...open on Sundays?	**Ist...sonntags geöffnet?**	ist...**zon**targs ger**urf**nert
When does it open?	**Wann wird geöffnet?**	vahn veert ger**urf**nert
When does it close?	**Wann schließt es?**	vahn shleest ehss
How much is the entrance fee?	**Was kostet der Eintritt?**	vahss **kos**tert derr **ighn**trit
Is there any reduction for...?	**Gibt es Ermäßigung für...?**	gipt ehss ehr**mais**sigung fewr
students/children	**Studenten/Kinder**	shtud**dehn**tern/**kind**err
Have you a guidebook (in English)?	**Haben Sie einen Führer (in Englisch)?**	**har**bern zee **igh**nern **few**rerr (in **ehng**lish)
Is it all right to take pictures?	**Darf man photographieren?**	dahrf mahn fottograh**fee**rern

EINTRITT FREI	ADMISSION FREE
PHOTOGRAPHIEREN VERBOTEN	NO CAMERAS ALLOWED

Who—What—When?

What's that building?	**Was für ein Gebäude ist das?**	vahss fewr ighn ger**boy**der ist dahss
Who was the...?	**Wer war der...?**	vayr varr derr
architect	**Architekt**	ahrkhit**tehkt**
artist	**Künstler**	**kewnst**lerr
painter	**Maler**	**mar**lerr
sculptor	**Bildhauer**	**bilt**howerr
Who built it?	**Wer hat es gebaut?**	vayr haht ehss ger**bowt**
Who painted that picture?	**Wer hat das Bild gemalt?**	vayr haht dahss bilt ger**marlt**
When did he live?	**Wann hat er gelebt?**	vahn haht ehr ger**laybt**
When was it built?	**Wann wurde es erbaut?**	vahn **woor**der ehss ehr**bowt**
Where's the house where...lived?	**Wo ist das Haus, in dem...wohnte?**	voa ist dahss howss in daym...**voan**ter
We're interested in...	**Wir interessieren uns für...**	veer intehreh**ssee**rern uns fewr
antiques	**Antiquitäten**	ahntikvit**tay**tern
archaeologie	**Archäologie**	ahrkhehoaloa**gee**
art	**Kunst**	kunst
botany	**Botanik**	bot**tar**nik
ceramics	**Keramik**	keh**rar**mik
coins	**Münzen**	**mewn**tsern
crafts	**Handwerk**	**hahnt**vehrk
fine arts	**bildende Künste**	**bil**dernder **kewn**ster
furniture	**Möbel**	**mur**berl
geology	**Geologie**	gayoaloa**gee**
history	**Geschichte**	ger**shikh**ter
medicine	**Medizin**	mehdi**tseen**
music	**Musik**	mu**zeek**
natural history	**Naturkunde**	nah**toor**kunder
ornithology	**Vogelkunde**	**foa**gerlkunder
painting	**Malerei**	marleh**righ**
pottery	**Töpferei**	turpfeh**righ**
prehistory	**Urgeschichte**	**oor**gershikhter
sculpture	**Bildhauerei**	**bilt**howerrigh
zoology	**Zoologie**	tsoaoaloa**gee**
Where's the...department?	**Wo ist die ...abteilung?**	voa ist dee...ahp**tigh**lung

SIGHTSEEING

Just the adjective you've been looking for...

It's...	**Es ist...**	ehss ist
amazing	**erstaunlich**	ehr**shtown**likh
awful	**scheußlich**	**shoyss**likh
beautiful	**schön**	shurn
gloomy	**düster**	**dew**sterr
impressive	**eindrucksvoll**	**ighn**druksfol
interesting	**interessant**	intehreh**ssahnt**
magnificent	**herrlich**	**hehr**likh
monumental	**großartig**	**groass**ahrtikh
overwhelming	**überwältigend**	ewberr**vehl**tiggernt
sinister	**unheimlich**	**un**highmlikh
strange	**seltsam**	**zehlt**zahm
superb	**hervorragend**	hehr**foar**rargernt
terrible	**schrecklich**	**shrehk**likh
terrifying	**entsetzlich**	ehnt**zehts**likh
tremendous	**außerordentlich**	owsserr**or**derntlikh
ugly	**häßlich**	**hehss**likh

Religious services

Most churches and cathedrals are open to the public except, of course, when a service is being conducted.

If you're interested in taking photographs, you should obtain permission first.

Services are conducted in English in many towns. Ask the local tourist office for further details.

Is there a... church near here?	**Gibt es eine... Kirche in der Nähe?**	gipt ehss **igh**ner... **keer**kher in derr **neh**er
Catholic	**katholische**	kah**toa**lisher
Protestant	**evangelische**	ehvahn**gay**lisher
At what time is...?	**Wann beginnt...?**	vahn ber**gint**
mass	**die Messe**	dee **meh**sser
the service	**der Gottesdienst**	derr **got**tersdeenst
Where can I find a...who speaks English?	**Wo finde ich einen..., der Englisch spricht?**	voa **fin**der ikh **igh**nern... derr **ehng**lish shprikht
priest/minister	**Priester/Pfarrer**	**pree**sterr/**pfah**rerr

SIGHTSEEING

Relaxing

Cinema (movies)—Theatre

Since cinema showings are seldom continuous, you can buy your tickets in advance. You can expect one feature film, a newsreel, perhaps a short documentary and numerous commercials. The matinée normally starts around 2 p.m. Theatre curtain time is about 8 p.m. Booking in advance is advisable.

You can find out what's playing from newspapers and billboards. In most large towns you can buy a publication of the type "This Week in...".

Have you a copy of "This Week in..."?	**Haben Sie einen «Veranstaltungs-kalender von...»?**	**har**bern zee **igh**nern feh**rahn**shtahltungskahlehn-derr fon
What's showing at the cinema tonight?	**Was gibt es heute abend im Kino zu sehen?**	vahss gipt ehss **hoy**ter **ar**bernt im **kee**noa tsu **zay**ern
What's playing at the...theatre?	**Was wird im ...theater gegeben?**	vahss veert im ...**tayar**terr ger**gay**bern
What sort of play is it?	**Was für ein Stück ist es?**	vahss fewr ighn shtewk ist ehss
Who's it by?	**Von wem ist es?**	fon vaym ist ehss
Can you recommend (a)...?	**Können Sie mir ...empfehlen?**	**kur**nern zee meer ...ehmp**fay**lern
good film	**einen guten Film**	**igh**nern **goo**tern film
comedy	**eine Komödie**	**igh**ner kommurdier
something light	**etwas Leichtes**	**eht**vahss **lighkh**ters
drama	**ein Drama**	ighn **drar**mar
musical	**ein Musical**	ighn "musical"
revue	**eine Revue**	**igh**ner reh**vew**
thriller	**einen Krimi**	**igh**nern **krim**mi
Western	**einen Western**	**igh**nern **veh**sterrn
At what theatre is that new play by...being performed?	**In welchem Theater wird das neue Stück von...gespielt?**	in **vehl**kherm tay**ar**terr veert dahss **noy**er shtewk fon...ger**shpeelt**

Where's that new film by... being shown?	**Wo läuft der neue Film von...?**	voa loyft derr **noy**er film fon
Who's in it?	**Wer spielt mit?**	vayr shpeelt mit
Who's the director?	**Wer ist der Regisseur?**	vayr it derr rehzhi**ssurr**
What time does the show begin?	**Wann beginnt die Vorstellung?**	vahn ber**gint** dee **foar**shtehlung
What time does the show end?	**Wann ist die Vorstellung zu Ende?**	vahn ist dee **foar**shtehlung tsu **ehn**der
What time does the first evening performance start?	**Um wieviel Uhr beginnt die erste Abendvorstellung?**	um **vee**feel oor ber**gint** dee **ehr**ster **ar**berntfoarshtehlung
Are there any tickets for tonight?	**Gibt es noch Karten für heute abend?**	gipt ehss nokh **kahr**tern fewr **hoy**ter **ar**bernt
How much are the tickets?	**Wie teuer sind die Karten?**	vee **toy**err zint dee **kahr**tern
I want to reserve 2 tickets for the show on Friday evening.	**Ich möchte 2 Karten für Freitag abend vorbestellen.**	ikh **murkh**ter 2 **kahr**tern fewr **frigh**targ **ar**bernt **foar**bershtehlern
Can I have a ticket for the matinée on Tuesday?	**Kann ich eine Karte für die Nachmittags-vorstellung am Dienstag bekommen?**	kahn ikh **igh**ner **kahr**ter fewr dee **nahkh**mittahgs-foarshtehlung ahm **deen**starg ber**kom**mern
I want a seat in the stalls (orchestra).	**Ich hätte gern einen Platz im Parkett.**	ikh **heh**ter gehrn **igh**nern plahts im pahr**keht**
Not too far back.	**Nicht zu weit hinten.**	nikht tsu vight **hin**tern
Somewhere in the middle.	**Irgendwo in der Mitte.**	**eer**gerntvoa in derr **mit**ter
How much are the seats in the circle (mezzanine)?	**Wie teuer sind die Plätze im ersten Rang?**	vee **toy**er zint dee **pleht**ser im **ehr**stern rahng
May I please have a programme?	**Kann ich bitte ein Programm haben?**	kahn ikh **bit**ter ighn pro**grahm** **har**bern
Can I check this coat?	**Kann ich den Mantel abgeben?**	kahn ikh dayn **mahn**terl **ahp**gaybern

Bedaure, es ist alles ausverkauft.	I'm sorry, we're sold out.
Es gibt nur noch ein paar Plätze im ersten Rang.	There are only a few seats left in the circle (mezzanine).
Darf ich Ihre Eintrittskarte sehen?	May I see your ticket?
Hier ist Ihr Platz.	This is your seat.

Opera—Ballet—Concert

Where's the opera house?	**Wo ist das Opernhaus?**	voa ist dahss **oa**perrnhowss
Is there an operetta playing this evening?	**Wird heute abend eine Operette gespielt?**	veert **hoy**ter **ar**bernt **igh**ner oaperr**eht**ter ger**shpeelt**
Where's the concert hall?	**Wo ist die Konzerthalle?**	voa ist dee kont**sehrt**hahler
What's on at the opera tonight?	**Was wird heute abend in der Oper gegeben?**	vahss veert **hoy**ter **ar**bernt in derr **oa**perr ger**gay**bern
Who's singing?	**Wer singt?**	vayr zingt
Who's dancing?	**Wer tanzt?**	vayr tahntst
What time does the programme start?	**Wann beginnt die Vorstellung?**	vahn ber**gint** dee **foar**shtehlung
What orchestra is playing?	**Welches Orchester spielt?**	**vehl**khers or**keh**sterr shpeelt
What are they playing?	**Was wird gespielt?**	vahss veert ger**shpeelt**
Who's the conductor?	**Wer ist der Dirigent?**	vayr ist derr dirri**gehnt**

Night-clubs

There are top night-clubs in major cities which are somewhat expensive. Find out the prices before you order—and allow for the various surcharges.

Night-time entertainment, however, is generally less showy, more intimate in Germany, Austria and Switzerland. Even in provincial towns you'll find a *Heuriger* (**hoy**rigerr), *Bierhalle* (**beer**hahler), *Bier-* or *Weinstube* (**vighn**shtoober) where a small band or orchestra may play light music from drinking songs to operatic airs. A costumed chorus often sings and encourages the customers to join in. Such a night spot is very popular and informal, a good place to meet the locals and inexpensive.

Can you recommend a good night-club?	**Können Sie ein gutes Nachtlokal empfehlen?**	**kur**nern zee ighn **goo**terss **nahkht**lokkarl ehm**pfay**lern
Is there a floor show?	**Gibt es Attraktionen?**	gipt ehss ahtrahk**tsioa**nern
What time does the floor show start?	**Wann beginnt das Programm?**	vahn ber**gint** dahss pro**grahm**
Is evening dress necessary?	**Wird Abendgarderobe verlangt?**	veert **ar**berntgahrdehroaber fehr**lahngt**

And once inside...

A table for 2, please.	**Einen Tisch für 2, bitte.**	**igh**nern tish fewr 2 **bit**ter
My name's... I reserved a table for 4.	**Ich heiße... Ich habe einen Tisch für 4 Personen reservieren lassen.**	ikh **high**sser..ikh **har**ber **igh**nern tish fewr 4 pehr**zoa**nern rehzerr**vee**rern **lah**ssern
I telephoned you earlier.	**Ich habe vor einer Weile angerufen.**	ikh **har**ber foar **igh**nerr **vigh**ler **ahn**gerroofern
We haven't got a reservation.	**Wir haben nicht reservieren lassen.**	veer **har**bern nikht rehzerr**vee**rern **lah**ssern

Dancing

Where can we go dancing?	**Wohin können wir tanzen gehen?**	voa**hin** **kur**nern veer **tahn**tsern **gay**ern
Is there a discotheque in town?	**Gibt es hier eine Diskothek?**	gipt ehss heer **igh**ner diskoa**thayk**
There's a dance at the...	**Im... findet ein Ball statt.**	im... findert ighn bahl shtaht
Would you like to dance?	**Darf ich bitten?**	dahrf ikh **bi**ttern
May I have this dance?	**Darf ich um diesen Tanz bitten?**	dahrf ikh um **dee**zern tahnts **bi**ttern

Do you happen to play...?

On a rainy day, this page may solve your problems.

Do you happen to play chess?	**Spielen Sie etwa Schach?**	**shpee**lern zee **eht**var shahkh
I'm afraid I don't.	**Leider nein.**	**ligh**derr nighn
No, but I'll give you a game of draughts (checkers).	**Nein, aber ich spiele mit Ihnen Dame.**	nighn **ar**berr ikh **shpee**ler mit **ee**nern **dar**mer
king	**der König**	derr **kur**nikh
queen	**die Dame**	dee **dar**mer
castle (rook)	**der Turm**	derr toorm
bishop	**der Läufer**	derr **loy**ferr
knight	**der Springer**	derr **shpring**err
pawn	**der Bauer**	derr **bow**err
Checkmate!	**Schachmatt!**	shahkh**maht**
Do you play cards?	**Spielen Sie Karten?**	**shpee**lern zee **kahr**tern
bridge	**Bridge**	"bridge"
gin rummy	**Rommé**	**rom**may
whist	**Whist**	"whist"
pontoon (21)	**Siebzehn und Vier**	**zeeb**tsayn unt feer
poker	**Poker**	**poa**kerr
hearts	**Herz**	kehrts
diamonds	**Karo**	**kar**roa
clubs	**Kreuz**	kroyts
spades	**Pik**	hehrts

RELAXING

ace	**das As**	dahss ahss
king	**der König**	derr **kurnikh**
queen	**die Dame**	dee **darmer**
jack	**der Bube**	derr **boober**
joker	**der Joker**	derr **joakerr**

Casino

You'll find casinos at most resorts and spas in Germany, Austria and Switzerland. Most stay open all year round but the usual season runs from Easter until mid-October.

Boule—similar to roulette—is the only game played in the modest casinos of Switzerland where the maximum stake is 5 francs in the game room.

To get into a casino, you'll need your passport. You must be over 21. You must also have a "clean record" in the gambling world. As far as you're concerned, you need have no doubts about the honesty of the game. All legitimate casinos are strictly controlled and regularly inspected. Casinos are anxious to avoid any risk of scandal or adverse public relations.

The minimum stake is usually the equivalent of a half-dollar (U.S.) or 20 pence. Entrance fees are nominal. The language of the casino is mostly German but the croupiers will understand enough English (or French) for your requirements.

For those who like to bet on horses there are a number of race courses. More modest gamblers can take advantage of some of the state-run football pools and lotteries.

FOR NUMBERS, see page 175

Sports

You name the sport, and you'll doubtless be able to find it in Germany, Austria and Switzerland. The most popular spectator sport is by far football (soccer).

Where's the nearest golf course?	**Wo ist der nächste Golfplatz?**	voa ist derr **nehkh**ster **golf**plahts
Can we hire (rent) clubs?	**Können wir Golfschläger leihen?**	**kur**nern veer **golf**shlaigerr **ligh**ern
Where are the tennis courts?	**Wo sind die Tennisplätze?**	voa zint dee **teh**nisplehtser
Can I hire rackets?	**Kann ich Tennisschläger leihen?**	kahn ikh **teh**nisshlaigerr **ligh**ern
What's the charge per...?	**Wieviel kostet es pro...?**	vee**feel kos**tert ehss proa
day/round/hour	**Tag/Runde/Stunde**	targ/**run**der/**shtun**der
Where's the nearest race course (track)?	**Wo ist die nächste Pferderennbahn?**	voa ist dee **nehkh**ster **pfehr**derrehnbarn
What's the admission charge?	**Was kostet der Eintritt?**	vahss **kos**tert derr **ighn**trit
Is there a swimming pool here?	**Gibt es hier ein Schwimmbad?**	gipt ehss heer ighn **shvim**bart
Is it open-air or indoors?	**Ist es ein Freibad oder ein Hallenbad?**	ist ehss ighn **frigh**bart oaderr ighn **hah**lernbart
Is it heated?	**Ist es geheizt?**	ist ehss ger**hightst**
Can one swim in the lake/river?	**Kann man im See/Fluß baden?**	kahn mahn im zay/fluss **bar**dern
I'd like to see a boxing match.	**Ich möchte gern einen Boxkampf sehen.**	ikh **murkh**ter gehrn **igh**nern **boks**kahmpf **zay**ern
Can you get me a couple of tickets?	**Können Sie mir zwei Karten besorgen?**	**kur**nern zee meer tsvigh **kahr**tern ber**zor**gern
Is there a football (soccer) game anywhere this Saturday?	**Findet diesen Samstag irgendwo ein Fußballspiel statt?**	**fin**dert **dee**zern **zahms**targ **ir**gerntvoa ighn **foos**bahlshpeel shtaht
Who's playing?	**Wer spielt?**	vayr shpeelt

Is there any good fishing around here?	**Kann man hier in der Nähe angeln?**	kahn mahn heer in derr naier **ahn**gerln
Do I need a permit?	**Brauche ich einen Angelschein?**	**brow**kher ikh **igh**nern **an**gerlshighn
Where can I get one?	**Wo bekomme ich einen?**	voa ber**kom**mer ikh **igh**nern

On the beach

Is it safe for swimming?	**Kann man hier ohne Gefahr schwimmen?**	kahn mahn heer **oa**ner ger**farr shvim**mern
Is there a lifeguard?	**Gibt es einen Rettungsdienst?**	gipt ehss **igh**nern **reh**tungsdeenst
The sea is very calm.	**Die See ist sehr ruhig.**	dee zay ist zayr **roo**ikh
There are some big waves.	**Die See geht recht hoch.**	dee zay gayt rehkht hoakh
Are there any dangerous currents?	**Gibt es gefährliche Strömungen?**	gipt ehss ger**fair**likher **shtrur**mungern
What time is high tide / low tide?	**Wann ist Flut/Ebbe?**	vahn ist floot / **eh**ber
What's the temperature of the water?	**Welche Temperatur hat das Wasser?**	**vehl**kher tehmperrah**toor** haht dahss **vah**sser
I want to hire a/an...	**Ich möchte... mieten.**	ikh **murkh**ter...**mee**tern
air mattress	**eine Luftmatratze**	**igh**ner **luft**mahtrahtser
bathing hut	**eine Badekabine**	**igh**ner **bar**derkarbeener
deck-chair	**einen Liegestuhl**	**igh**nern **lee**gershtool
skin-diving equipment	**eine Tauchausrüstung**	**igh**ner **towkh**owsrewstung
sunshade	**einen Sonnenschirm**	**igh**nern **zon**nernsheerm
surfboard	**ein Brett zum Wellenreiten**	ighn breht tsum **veh**lernrightern
tent	**ein Zelt**	ighn tsehlt
some water-skis	**Wasserschi**	**vah**sserrshee

PRIVATSTRAND	BADEN VERBOTEN
PRIVATE BEACH	NO BATHING

RELAXING

Where can I rent a...?	**Wo kann ich... mieten?**	voa kahn ikh...meetern
canoe	**ein Paddelboot**	ighn pahderlboat
motor-boat	**ein Motorboot**	ighn moatorboat
rowing-boat	**ein Ruderboot**	ighn rooderrboat
sailing-boat	**ein Segelboot**	ighn zaygerlboat
What's the charge per hour?	**Was kostet es pro Stunde?**	vahss kostert ehss proa shtunder

Winter sports

Austria and Switzerland are particularly well-known for their ski resorts (some of them operate year round), and both countries contend for the merit of having originated modern skiing. Germany, too, has many well-equipped resorts. For the beginner there are excellent ski schools. Skiing equipment can be hired everywhere, not only in the resorts but also in most sporting goods shops in the cities. Curling, ice-hockey and skating are also widely practiced.

Is there a skating-rink near here?	**Gibt es hier in der Nähe eine Eisbahn?**	gipt ehss heer in derr naier ighner ighsbarn
What are the skiing conditions like at...?	**Wie sind die Schneeverhältnisse in...?**	vee zint dee shnayfehr-hehltnisser in
Can I take skiing lessons there?	**Kann ich dort Schiunterricht nehmen?**	kahn ikh dort sheeunterrikht naymern
Are there ski lifts?	**Gibt es dort Schilifts?**	gipt ehss dort sheelifts
I want to hire a/some...	**Ich möchte... mieten.**	ikh murkhter... meetern
ice skates	**Schlittschuhe**	shlitshooer
skiing equipment	**eine Schiausrüstung**	ighner sheeowssrewstung
toboggan	**einen Rodelschlitten**	ighnern roaderlshlittern
sled	**einen Schlitten**	ighnern shlittern
boots	**Stiefel**	shteeferl
poles	**Schistöcke**	sheesturker
skis	**Schier**	sheeerr

Camping—Countryside

In many parts of Germany, camping isn't allowed without a permit. There are plenty of authorized camping sites, some with excellent facilities.

If you want to be on the safe side, choose a site that is recognized by the ADAC *(Allgemeiner Deutscher Automobil Club)*. There are over 700 of them. Switzerland and Austria also have well-equipped camping sites, some of them high up in the mountains. There are numerous youth hostels—for information, apply to the national youth hostels organizations.

If you want to camp on private land, get permission from the owner first.

Can we camp here?	**Können wir hier zelten?**	kurnern veer heer tsehltern
Where can we camp for the night?	**Wo können wir heute nacht zelten?**	voa kurnern veer hoyter nahkht tsehltern
Is there a camping site near here?	**Gibt es hier in der Nähe einen Campingplatz?**	gipt ehss heer in derr nayer ighnern kehmpingplahts
May we camp in your field?	**Dürfen wir auf Ihrer Wiese zelten?**	dewrfern veer owf eererr veezer tsehltern
Can we park our caravan (trailer) here?	**Dürfen wir unseren Wohnwagen hier abstellen?**	dewrfern veer unzerrern voanvargern heer ahpshtehlern
Is this an official camping site?	**Ist dies ein offizieller Campingplatz?**	ist deess ighn ofitsiehlerr kehmpingplahts
May we light a fire?	**Dürfen wir ein Feuer machen?**	dewrfern veer ighn foyerr mahkhern
Is there drinking water?	**Gibt es Trinkwasser?**	gipt ehss trinkvahsserr
Are there shopping facilities on the site?	**Gibt es Einkaufsmöglichkeiten auf dem Platz?**	gipt ehss ighnkowfsmurglikhkightern owf daym plahts

Are there...?	**Gibt es...?**	gipt ehss
baths	**Bäder**	**bai**derr
showers	**Duschen**	**doo**shern
toilets	**Toiletten**	toah**leh**tern
What's the charge...?	**Wie hoch sind die Gebühren...?**	vee hoakh zint dee ger**bew**rern
per day	**pro Tag**	proa targ
per person	**pro Person**	proa pehr**zoan**
for a car	**pro Wagen**	proa **var**gern
for a caravan (trailer)	**pro Wohnwagen**	proa **voan**vargern
for a tent	**pro Zelt**	proa tsehlt
Is there a youth hostel near here?	**Gibt es hier irgendwo eine Jugendherberge?**	gipt ehss heer **eer**gerntvoa **igh**ner **yoo**gernthehrbehrger
Do you know anyone who can put us up for the night?	**Kennen Sie jemanden, der uns heute nacht aufnehmen könnte?**	**keh**nern zee **yay**mahndern derr uns **hoy**ter nahkht **owf**naymern **kurn**ter

ZELTEN VERBOTEN	KEINE WOHNWAGEN
NO CAMPING	NO CARAVANS (TRAILERS)

Landmarks

barn	**die Scheune**	dee **shoy**ner
beach	**der Strand**	derr shtrahnt
bridge	**die Brücke**	dee **brew**ker
brook	**der Bach**	derr bahkh
building	**das Gebäude**	dahss ger**boy**der
canal	**der Kanal**	derr kah**narl**
castle	**die Burg/das Schloß**	dee boorg / dahss shloss
church	**die Kirche**	dee **keer**kher
cliff	**die Felswand**	dee **fehls**vahnt
copse	**das Gehölz**	dahss ger**hurlts**
cottage	**das Häuschen**	dahss **hoys**khern
crossroads	**die Straßenkreuzung**	dee **shtrar**ssernkroytsung
farm	**der Bauernhof**	derr **bow**errnhoaf
ferry	**die Fähre**	dee **fai**rer
field	**das Feld**	dahss fehlt
footpath	**der Fußweg**	derr **foos**svayg
forest	**der Wald**	derr vahlt
fortress	**die Festung**	dee **feh**stung

hamlet	**der Weiler**	derr **vigh**lerr
heath	**die Heide**	dee **high**der
highway	**die Landstraße**	dee **lahnt**shtrarsser
hill	**der Hügel**	derr **hew**gerl
house	**das Haus**	dahss howss
hut	**die Hütte**	dee **hew**ter
inn	**das Gasthaus**	dahss **gahst**howss
lake	**der See**	derr zay
marsh	**das Moor**	dahss moar
moorland	**das Heidemoor**	dahss **high**dermoar
mountain	**der Berg**	derr behrg
mountain range	**die Gebirgskette**	dee ger**beergs**kehter
path	**der Pfad**	derr pfart
peak	**die Bergspitze**	dee **behrg**shpitser
pond	**der Weiher**	derr **vigh**err
pool	**der Teich**	derr tighkh
railway track	**das Eisenbahngleis**	dahss **igh**zernbarn-glighss
river	**der Fluß**	derr fluss
road	**die Straße**	dee **shtrar**sser
ruin	**die Ruine**	dee rueener
sea	**die See/das Meer**	dee zay/dahss mayr
spring	**die Quelle**	dee **kveh**ler
stream	**der Bach**	derr bahkh
swamp	**der Sumpf**	derr zumpf
tower	**der Turm**	derr toorm
track	**der Feldweg**	derr **fehlt**vayg
tree	**der Baum**	derr bowm
valley	**das Tal**	dahss tarl
village	**das Dorf**	dahss doarf
vineyard	**der Weinberg**	derr **vighn**behrg
water	**das Gewässer**	dahss ger**veh**sserr
waterfall	**der Wasserfall**	derr **vah**sserrfahl
water tower	**der Wasserturm**	derr **vah**sserrtoorm
well	**der Brunnen**	derr **brun**nern
wood	**der Wald**	derr vahlt
What's the name of that river?	**Wie heißt dieser Fluß?**	vee highst **dee**zerr fluss
How high is that mountain?	**Wie hoch ist dieser Berg?**	vee hoakh ist **dee**zerr behrg

...and if you're tired of walking, you can always try hitchhiking—though you may have to wait a long time for a lift.

Can you give me a lift to...?	**Können Sie mich nach ... mitnehmen?**	**kur**nern zee mikh nahkh ...**mit**naymern

FOR ASKING THE WAY, see page 144

Making friends

Introductions

Here are a few phrases to get you started:

How do you do?	**Guten Tag.**	**goo**tern targ
How are you?	**Wie geht es Ihnen?**	vee gayt ehss **ee**nern
Very well, thank you.	**Danke, sehr gut.**	**dahng**ker zayr goot
How's life?	**Wie geht's?**	vee gayts
Fine, thanks. And you?	**Danke gut, und Ihnen?**	**dang**ker goot unt **ee**nern
May I introduce Miss Philips?	**Darf ich Fräulein Philips vorstellen?**	dahrf ikh **froy**lighn Philips **foar**shtehlern
I'd like you to meet a friend of mine.	**Ich möchte Sie mit einem Freund von mir bekanntmachen.**	ikh **murkh**ter zee mit **igh**nerm froynt fon meer ber**kahnt**mahkhern
John, this is...	**John, das ist...**	John dahss ist
My name's...	**Ich heiße...**	ikh **high**sser
Glad to know you.	**Sehr erfreut.**	zayr ehr**froyt**

Follow-up

How long have you been here?	**Wie lange sind Sie schon hier?**	vee **lahng**er zint zee shoan heer
We've been here a week.	**Wir sind seit einer Woche hier.**	veer zint zight **igh**nerr **vo**kher heer
Is this your first visit?	**Ist es Ihr erster Besuch?**	ist ehss eer **ehr**sterr beh**zookh**
No, we came here last year.	**Nein, wir waren schon letztes Jahr hier.**	nighn veer **var**rern shoan **lehts**terss yarr heer
Are you enjoying your stay?	**Gefällt es Ihnen hier?**	ger**fehlt** ehss **ee**nern heer

Yes, I like...very much.	**Ja, mir gefällt... sehr gut.**	yar meer ger**fehlt**... zayr goot
Are you on your own?	**Sind Sie allein hier?**	zint zee ah**lighn** heer
I'm with...	**Ich bin mit...**	ikh bin mit
my wife	**meiner Frau**	**migh**nerr frow
my husband	**meinem Mann**	**migh**nerm mahn
my family	**meiner Familie**	**migh**nerr fah**mee**lier
my parents	**meinen Eltern**	**migh**nern **ehl**terrn
some friends	**ein paar Freunden**	ighn parr **froyn**dern
Where do you come from?	**Woher kommen Sie?**	voa**hayr kom**mern zee
What part of...do you come from?	**Aus welcher Gegend von...kommen Sie?**	owss **vehl**kherr **gay**gernt fon...**kom**mern zee
I'm from...	**Ich bin aus...**	ikh bin owss
Where are you staying?	**Wo wohnen Sie?**	voa **voa**nern zee
I'm a student.	**Ich bin Student.**	ikh bin shtud**dehnt**
What are you studying?	**Was studieren Sie?**	vahss shtud**dee**rern zee
We're here on holiday.	**Wir machen Ferien hier.**	veer **mah**khern **fay**riern heer
I'm here on a business trip.	**Ich bin auf einer Geschäftsreise hier.**	ikh bin owf **igh**nerr ger**shehfts**righzer heer
What kind of business are you in?	**In welcher Branche sind Sie?**	in **vehl**kherr **brahng**sher zint zee
What's your occupation?	**Was sind Sie von Beruf?**	vahss zint zee fon ber**roof**
I hope we'll see you again soon.	**Ich hoffe, daß wir Sie bald wiedersehen.**	ikh **hof**fer dahss veer zee bahlt **vee**derrzayern
See you later.	**Bis später.**	biss **shpai**terr
See you tomorrow	**Bis morgen.**	biss **mor**gern

The weather

They talk about the weather just as much in Germany as the Americans and British are supposed to do. So...

What a lovely day!	**Was für ein herrlicher Tag!**	vahss fewr ighn **hehr**likherr targ
What awful weather.	**Was für ein scheußliches Wetter.**	vahss fewr ighn **shoys**likherss **veh**terr
Isn't it cold today?	**Welche Kälte heute!**	**vehl**kher **kehl**ter **hoy**ter
Isn't it hot today?	**Welche Hitze heute!**	**vehl**kher **hit**ser **hoy**ter
Is it usually as warm as this?	**Ist es immer so warm?**	ist ehss **imm**err zoa vahrm
It's very foggy, isn't it?	**Es ist recht neblig, nicht wahr?**	ehss ist rehkht **nay**blikh nikht varr
Do you think it'll... tomorrow?	**Glauben Sie, es wird morgen...?**	**glow**bern zee ehss veert **mor**gern
rain	**regnen**	**rayg**nern
be sunny	**sonnig sein**	**son**nikh zighn
snow	**schneien**	**shnigh**ern
clear up	**aufklaren**	**owf**klahrern

Invitations

My wife and I would like you to dine with us on...	**Meine Frau und ich würden Sie gern am... zum Abendessen einladen.**	**migh**ner frow unt ikh **vewr**dern zee gehrn ahm... tsum **ar**berntehssern **ighn**lardern
Can you come to dinner tomorrow night?	**Können Sie morgen zum Abendessen kommen?**	**kur**nern zee **mor**gern tsum **ar**berntehssern **kom**mern
We're giving a small party tomorrow night. I do hope you can come.	**Wir geben morgen abend eine kleine Party. Ich hoffe, Sie können kommen.**	veer **gay**bern **mor**gern **ar**bernt **igh**ner **kligh**ner **par**rtee. ikh **hof**fer zee **kur**nern **kom**mern
Can you come over for cocktails this evening?	**Können Sie heute abend auf ein Gläschen zu uns kommen?**	**kur**nern zee **hoy**ter **ar**bernt owf ighn **glais**khern tsu uns **kom**mern

There's a party. Are you coming?	**Es findet eine Party statt. Kommen Sie auch?**	ehss **fin**dert **igh**ner **parr**tee shtaht. **kom**mern zee owkh
That's very kind of you.	**Das ist sehr nett von Ihnen.**	dahss ist zayr neht fon **ee**nern
Great. I'd love to come.	**Prima, ich komme sehr gerne.**	**pree**mar ikh **kom**mer zayr **gehr**ner
What time shall we come?	**Wann sollen wir da sein?**	vahn **zol**lern veer dar zighn
May I bring a friend?	**Kann ich einen Freund mit-bringen?**	kahn ikh **igh**nern froynt **mit**bringern
May I bring a girl friend?	**Kann ich eine Freun-din mitbringen?**	kahn ikh **igh**ner **froyn**din **mit**bringern
I'm afraid we've got to go now.	**Leider müssen wir jetzt gehen.**	**ligh**derr **mew**ssern veer yehtst **gay**ern
Next time you must come to visit us.	**Nächstes Mal müssen Sie uns besuchen.**	**nehkh**sterss marl **mew**ssern zee uns ber**zoo**khern
Thanks for the evening. It was great.	**Vielen Dank für den Abend, es war herrlich.**	**fee**lern dahngk fewr dayn **ar**bernt ehss varr **hehr**likh

Dating

Would you like a cigarette?	**Darf ich Ihnen eine Zigarette anbieten?**	dahrf ikh **ee**nern **igh**ner tsiggah**reh**ter **ahn**beetern
Do you have a light, please?	**Können Sie mir bitte Feuer geben?**	**kur**nern zee meer **bit**ter **foy**err **gay**bern
Can I get you a drink?	**Darf ich Ihnen etwas zu trinken bestellen?**	dahrf ikh **ee**nern **eht**vahss tsu **tring**kern ber**steh**lern
Excuse me, could you please help me?	**Verzeihung, könnten Sie mir bitte helfen?**	fehr**tsigh**ung **kurn**tern zee meer **bit**ter **hehl**fern
I'm lost. Can you show me the way to...?	**Ich habe mich verlaufen. Können Sie mir den Weg zur/zum ... zeigen?**	ikh **har**ber mikh fehr**low**fern. **kur**nern zee meer dayn vayg tsoor/tsum... **tsigh**gern
Are you waiting for someone?	**Warten Sie auf jemanden?**	**vahr**tern zee owf **yay**mahndern

MAKING FRIENDS

Are you free this evening?	**Sind Sie heute abend frei?**	zint zee **hoyter arbernt** frigh
Would you like to go out with me tonight?	**Würden Sie heute abend mit mir ausgehen?**	**vewr**dern zee **hoyter arbernt** mit meer **ows**gayern
Would you like to go dancing?	**Würden Sie gern tanzen gehen?**	**vewr**dern zee gehrn **tahn**tsern **gay**ern
I know a good discotheque.	**Ich kenne eine gute Diskothek.**	ikh **keh**ner **igh**ner **goo**ter disko**a**tayk
Shall we go to the cinema (movies)?	**Wollen wir ins Kino gehen?**	**vo**llern veer ins **kee**noa **gay**ern
Would you like to go for a drive?	**Wollen wir ein bißchen durch die Gegend fahren?**	**vo**llern veer ighn **biss**khern doorkh dee **gay**gernt **far**rern
I'd love to, thank you.	**Danke, sehr gern.**	**dahng**ker zayr gehrn
Where shall we meet?	**Wo treffen wir uns?**	voa **treh**fern veer uns
I'll pick you up at your hotel.	**Ich hole Sie in Ihrem Hotel ab.**	ikh **hoa**ler zee in **ee**rerm hoa**tehl** ahp
I'll call for you at 8.	**Ich hole Sie um 8 Uhr ab.**	ikh **hoa**ler zee um 8 oor ahp
May I take you home?	**Darf ich Sie nach Hause bringen?**	dahrf ikh zee nahkh **how**zer **bring**ern
Can I see you again tomorrow?	**Darf ich Sie morgen wiedersehen?**	dahrf ikh zee **mor**gern **vee**derrzayern
Thank you, it's been a wonderful evening.	**Danke, es war ein wunderbarer Abend.**	**dahng**ker ehss varr ighn **vun**derrbarrerr **arbernt**
I've enjoyed myself tremendously.	**Ich habe mich sehr gut amüsiert.**	ikh **har**ber mikh zayr goot ahmew**zeert**
What's your telephone number?	**Wie ist Ihre Telephonnummer?**	vee ist **ee**rer tehleh**foan**nummerr
Do you live alone?	**Wohnen Sie allein?**	**voa**nern zee ah**lighn**
What time is your last train?	**Wann geht Ihr letzter Zug?**	vahn gayt eer **lehts**terr tsoog

Shopping guide

This shopping guide is designed to help you find what you want with ease, accuracy and speed. It features:

1. a list of all major shops, stores and services (p. 98)
2. some general expressions required when shopping to allow you to be specific and selective (p. 100)
3. full details of the shops and services most likely to concern you. Here you'll find advice, alphabetical lists of items and conversion charts listed under the headings below.

		Page
Bookshop	books, magazines, newpapers, stationery	104
Camping	camping equipment	106
Chemist's (drugstore)	medicine, first-aid, cosmetics, toilet articles	108
Clothing	clothes, shoes, accessories	112
Electrical appliances	radios, tape-recorders, shavers, records	119
Hairdresser's	barber's, ladies' hairdresser's, beauty salon	121
Jeweller's	jewellery, watches, watch repairs	123
Laundry/Dry cleaning	usual facilities	126
Photography	cameras, accessories, films, developing	127
Provisions	this is confined to basic items required for picnics	129
Souvenirs	souvenirs, gifts, fancy goods	131
Tobacconist's	smoker's supplies	132

Shops, stores and services

If you've a clear idea of what you want before you set out, then look under the appropriate heading, pick out the article and find a suitable description for it (colour, material, etc.).

German shops usually open at around 8 a.m. and close at 6.30 p.m.; some close for lunch. On Saturdays shops close at 2 p.m., except on the first Saturday of the month when they're open until 6 p.m.

In Vienna, shops are open weekdays from 8 or 9 a.m. to 6 p.m., sometimes closing at noon for two or three hours. Stores close at 12.30 p.m. on Saturday. In other Austrian cities, shops often take a lunch break while evening closing hours vary.

Swiss shop hours are usually 8 a.m. to 6.30 p.m. with a two-hour lunch break. In some regions, shops close at 1 p.m. on Saturdays while in other localities shops remain open until 5 p.m.

Where's the nearest...?	**Wo ist der/die/das nächste...?**	voa ist derr/dee/dahss **nehkh**ster
antique shop	**das Antiquitätengeschäft**	dahss ahntikvit**tay**terngershehft
art gallery	**die Kunstgalerie**	dee **kunst**gahlehree
baker's	**die Bäckerei**	dee behker**righ**
bank	**die Bank**	dee bahngk
barber's	**der Friseur**	derr fri**zurr**
beauty salon	**der Kosmetiksalon**	derr kos**may**tikzahlong
bookshop	**die Buchhandlung**	dee **bukh**hahntlung
butcher's	**die Fleischerei/ Metzgerei**	dee **fligh**sherrigh/ **mehts**gerrigh
candy store	**der Süßwarenladen**	derr **sews**varrernlardern
chemist's	**die Apotheke**	dee ahpoa**tay**ker
confectioner's	**die Konditorei**	dee konditoa**righ**
dairy shop	**die Milchhandlung**	dee milkhhahntlung
delicatessen	**das Delikatessengeschäft**	dahss dehlikkah**teh**sserngershehft
dentist	**der Zahnarzt**	derr **tsarn**ahrtst
department store	**das Warenhaus**	dahss **var**rernhowss
doctor	**der Arzt**	derr ahrtst

drugstore	**die Apotheke**	dee ahpoa**tay**ker
dry cleaner's	**die chemische Reinigung**	dee **khay**misher **righ**nigung
fishmonger's	**die Fischhandlung**	dee **fish**hahntlung
furrier's	**das Pelzgeschäft**	dahss **pehlts**gershehft
florist's	**das Blumengeschäft**	dahss **bloo**merngershehft
greengrocer's	**die Gemüsehandlung**	dee ger**mew**zerhahntlung
grocery	**das Lebensmittelgeschäft**	dahss **lay**bernsmitterlgershehft
hairdresser's (ladies)	**der Damenfriseur**	derr **dar**mernfrizurr
hardware store	**die Eisenwarenhandlung**	dee **igh**zernvarrernhahntlung
health food shop	**das Reformhaus**	dahss reh**form**howss
hospital	**das Krankenhaus**	dahss **krahng**kernhowss
jeweller's	**der Juwelier**	derr yuveh**leer**
launderette	**der Waschsalon**	derr **vahsh**zahlong
laundry	**die Wäscherei**	dee vehsher**righ**
liquor store	**die Spirituosenhandlung**	dee shpirritu**oa**zernhahntlung
market	**der Markt**	derr mahrkt
news-stand	**der Zeitungsstand**	derr **tsigh**tungsshtahnt
off-licence	**die Spirituosenhandlung**	dee shpirritu**oa**zernhahntlung
optician	**der Optiker**	derr **op**tikkerr
pastry shop	**die Konditorei**	dee kondittoa**righ**
photo shop	**das Photogeschäft**	dahss **foa**toagershehft
police station	**die Polizeiwache**	dee polit**sigh**vahkher
post office	**das Postamt**	dahss **post**ahmt
shoe shop	**das Schuhgeschäft**	dahss **shoo**gershehft
shoemaker's (repairs)	**der Schuhmacher**	derr **shoo**mahkherr
souvenir shop	**der Andenkenladen**	derr **ahn**dehngkernlardern
sporting goods shop	**das Sportgeschäft**	dahss **shport**gershehft
stationer's	**das Schreibwarengeschäft**	dahss **shrighp**varrerngershehft
supermarket	**der Supermarkt**	derr **zoo**perrmahrkt
sweet shop	**der Süßwarenladen**	derr **zews**varrernlardern
tailor's	**der Herrenschneider**	derr **heh**rernshnighderr
telegraph office	**das Telegraphenamt**	dahss tehleh**grar**fernahmt
tobacconist's	**der Tabakladen**	derr tah**bahk**lardern
toy shop	**das Spielwarengeschäft**	dahss **shpeel**varrerngershehft
travel agent	**das Reisebüro**	dahss **righ**zerbewroa
vegetable store	**die Gemüsehandlung**	dee ger**mew**zerhahntlung
veterinarian	**der Tierarzt**	derr **teer**ahrtst
watchmaker's	**der Uhrmacher**	derr **oor**mahkherr
wine merchant's	**die Weinhandlung**	dee **vighn**hahntlung

General expressions

Here are some expressions which will be useful to you when you're out shopping:

Where?

Where's a good...?	**Wo ist ein guter...?**	voa ist ighn **goo**terr
Where can I find...?	**Wo finde ich...?**	voa **fin**der ikh
Where do they sell...?	**Wo bekomme ich...?**	voa ber**kom**mer ikh
Can you recommend an inexpensive...?	**Können Sie einen preiswerten... empfehlen?**	**kur**nern zee **ighn**ern **prighs**vayrtern... ehm**pfay**lern
Where's the main shopping area?	**Wo ist das Geschäftsviertel?**	voa ist dahss ger**shehfts**feerterl
How far is it from here?	**Wie weit ist es von hier?**	vee vight ist ehss fon heer
How do I get there?	**Wie komme ich dorthin?**	vee **kom**mer ikh dorthin

Service

Can you help me?	**Können Sie mir helfen?**	**kur**nern zee meer **hehl**fern
I'm just looking around.	**Ich sehe mich nur um.**	ikh **zay**er mikh noor um
I want...	**Ich hätte gern...**	ikh **heh**ter gehrn
Can you show me some...?	**Können Sie mir einige... zeigen?**	**kur**nern zee meer **igh**nigger...**tsigh**gern
Do you have any...?	**Haben Sie...?**	**har**bern zee

That one

Can you show me...?	**Können Sie mir... zeigen?**	**kur**nern zee meer... **tsigh**gern
that/those	**das/diese**	dahss/**dee**zer
the one in the window	**das im Schaufenster**	dahss im **show**fehnsterr
the one in the display case	**das in der Vitrine**	dahss in derr vi**tree**ner
It's over there.	**Es ist dort drüben.**	ehss ist dort **drew**bern

SHOPPING GUIDE

Defining the article

I'd like a...	**Ich hätte gern...**	ikh **hehter** gehrn
It must be...	**Es muß...sein.**	ehss muss...zighn
big	**groß**	groass
cheap	**billig**	**bil**likh
dark	**dunkel**	**dun**kerl
good	**gut**	goot
heavy	**schwer**	shvayr
large	**groß**	groass
light (weight)	**leicht**	lighkht
light (colour)	**hell**	hehl
oval	**oval**	oa**varl**
rectangular	**rechteckig**	**rehkht**ehkikh
round	**rund**	runt
small	**klein**	klighn
square	**quadratisch**	kvahlit**tait**
I don't want anything too expensive.	**Ich möchte nichts all zu Teures.**	ikh **murkh**ter nikhts ahll tsu **toy**rerss

Preference

I prefer something of better quality.	**Ich hätte lieber eine bessere Qualität.**	ikh **hehter lee**berr **igh**ner **beh**sserer kvahlit**tait**
Can you show me some more?	**Können Sie mir bitte mehr zeigen?**	**kur**nern zee meer **bit**ter mayr **tsigh**gern
Haven't you anything...?	**Haben Sie nicht etwas...?**	**har**bern zee nikht eht**vahss**
cheaper/better	**Billigeres/Besseres**	**bil**ligerrerss / **beh**sserrerss
larger/smaller	**Größeres/Kleineres**	**grur**sserrerss / **kligh**nerrerss

How much?

How much is this?	**Wieviel kostet das?**	vee**feel ko**stert dahss
How much are they?	**Wieviel kosten sie?**	vee**feel ko**stern zee
I don't understand.	**Ich verstehe nicht.**	ikh fehr**shtay**er nikht
Please write it down.	**Schreiben Sie es bitte auf.**	**shrigh**bern zee ehss **bit**ter owf
I don't want to spend more than 20 marks.	**Ich möchte nicht mehr als 20 Mark ausgeben.**	ikh **murkh**ter nikht mayr ahls 20 mahrk **ows**gaybern

FOR COLOURS, see page 113

Decision

That's just what I want.	**Das ist genau das, was ich möchte.**	dahss ist ger**now** dahss vahss ikh **murkh**ter
It's not quite what I want.	**Es ist nicht ganz das, was ich möchte.**	ehss ist nikht gahnts dahss vahss ikh **murkh**ter
No, I don't like it.	**Nein, das gefällt mir nicht.**	nighn dahss ger**fehlt** meer nikht
I'll take it.	**Ich nehme es.**	ikh **nay**mer ehss

Ordering

Can you order it for me?	**Können Sie es mir bestellen?**	**kur**nern zee ehss meer ber**shteh**lern
How long will it take?	**Wie lange dauert es?**	vee **lahn**ger **dow**errt ehss
I'd like it as soon as possible.	**Ich hätte es gern so schnell wie möglich.**	ikh **heh**ter ehss gehrn zoa shnehl vee **murg**likh

Delivery

I'll take it with me.	**Ich nehme es mit.**	ikh **nay**mer ehss mit
Deliver it to the... Hotel.	**Liefern Sie es bitte ins Hotel...**	**lee**ferrn zee ehss **bit**ter ins hoa**tehl**
Please send it to this address.	**Senden Sie es bitte an diese Adresse.**	**zehn**dern zee ehss **bit**ter ahn **dee**zer ah**dreh**sser
Will I have any difficulty with customs?	**Werde ich Schwierigkeiten mit dem Zoll haben?**	**vayr**der ikh **shvee**rikhkightern mit daym tsol **har**bern

Paying

How much is it?	**Wieviel kostet es?**	vee**feel ko**stert ehss
Can I pay by traveller's cheque?	**Kann ich mit einem Reisescheck bezahlen?**	kahn ikh mit **igh**nerm **righ**zershehk ber**tsar**lern
Do you accept dollars/pounds?	**Nehmen Sie Dollar/ Pfund an?**	naymern zee **dol**lahr/ pfunt ahn
Do you accept credit cards?	**Nehmen Sie Kreditkarten an?**	**nay**mern zee kray**dit**kahrtern ahn

Haven't you made a mistake in the bill?	**Haben Sie sich nicht verrechnet?**	**har**bern zee zikh nikht fehr**rehkh**nert
Do you have a carrier (shopping) bag?	**Haben Sie eine Tragetasche?**	**har**bern zee **igh**ner **trar**gertahsher
Would you please gift wrap it?	**Würden Sie es bitte als Geschenk einpacken?**	**vewr**dern zee ehss **bit**ter ahlss ger**shehngk** **ighn**pahkern

Dissatisfied

Can you please exchange this?	**Können Sie das bitte umtauschen?**	**kur**nern zee dahss **bit**ter umtowshern
I want to return this.	**Ich möchte das zurückgeben.**	ikh **murkh**ter dahss tsoo**rewk**gaybern
I'd like a refund. Here's the receipt.	**Ich möchte das Geld zurückerstattet haben. Hier ist die Quittung.**	ikh **murkh**ter dahss gehlt tsoo**rewk**ehrshtahtert **har**bern. heer ist dee **kvit**tung

Kann ich Ihnen helfen?	Can I help you?
Was hätten Sie gerne?	What would you like?
Welche...möchten Sie?	What...would you like?
Farbe/Form Qualität/Menge	colour/shape quality/quantity
Es tut mir leid, das haben wir nicht.	I'm sorry, we haven't any.
Das haben wir nicht vorrätig.	We're out of stock.
Sollen wir es für Sie bestellen?	Shall we order it for you?
Nehmen Sie es mit oder sollen wir es Ihnen senden?	Will you take it with you or shall we send it?
Sonst noch etwas?	Anything else?
Das macht... Mark, bitte.	That's...marks, please.
Die Kasse ist dort drüben.	The cashier's over there.

Bookshop—Stationer's—News-stand

In Germany, bookshops and stationers' are usually separate shops, though the latter will often sell paperbacks. Newspapers and magazines are sold at news-stands.

Where's the nearest...?	**Wo ist der/die/das nächste...?**	voa ist derr/dee/dahss **neh**khster
bookshop	**die Buchhandlung**	dee **bukh**hahntlung
stationer's	**das Schreibwarengeschäft**	dahss **shrighp**varrern-gershehft
news-stand	**der Zeitungsstand**	derr **tsigh**tungsshtahnt
Where can I buy an English-language newspaper?	**Wo kann ich eine englische Zeitung bekommen?**	voa kahn ikh **igh**ner **ehng**lisher **tsigh**tung ber**kom**mern
I want to buy a/an/some...	**Ich möchte...**	ikh **murkh**ter
address book	**ein Adressenbüchlein**	ighn ah**drehs**sern-bewkhlighn
ball-point pen	**einen Kugelschreiber**	**igh**nern **koo**gerlshrighberr
book	**ein Buch**	ighn bukh
box of paints	**einen Farbkasten**	**igh**nern **fahrp**kahstern
carbon paper	**Durchschlagpapier**	**doorkh**shlargpahpeer
cellophane tape	**durchsichtigen Klebestreifen**	**doorkh**sikhtiggern **klay**bershtrighfern
crayons	**Farbstifte**	**fahrp**shtifter
dictionary	**ein Wörterbuch**	ighn **vurr**terrbookh
German-English	**deutsch-englisch**	doych-**ehng**lish
pocket dictionary	**ein Taschenwörterbuch**	ighn **tah**shernvurrterr-bookh
drawing paper	**Zeichenpapier**	**tsigh**khernpahpeer
drawing pins	**Reißzwecken**	**righs**tsvehkern
envelopes	**Briefumschläge**	**breef**umshlaiger
eraser	**einen Radiergummi**	**igh**nern rah**deer**gummi
exercise book	**ein Schreibheft**	ighn **shrighp**hehft
fountain pen	**einen Füllfederhalter**	**igh**nern **fewl**fayderrhahlterr
glue	**Leim**	lighm
grammar book	**eine Grammatik**	**igh**ner grah**mah**tik
guide-book	**einen Reiseführer**	**igh**nern **righ**zerfewrerr
ink	**Tinte**	**tin**ter
black/red/blue	**schwarz/rot/blau**	shvahrts/roat/blow
labels	**Etikette**	ehti**keh**ter
magazine	**eine Illustrierte**	**igh**ner illus**treer**ter

SHOPPING GUIDE

map	**eine Landkarte**	igh**ner lahnt**kahrter
map of the town	**einen Stadtplan**	**igh**nern **shtaht**plarn
road map of...	**eine Straßenkarte von...**	**igh**ner **shtrar**ssernkahrter fon
newspaper	**eine Zeitung**	**igh**ner **tsigh**tung
American	**amerikanische**	ahmehri**kar**nisher
English	**englische**	**ehng**lisher
notebook	**ein Notizheft**	ighn **nottitshehft**
note paper	**Briefpapier**	**breef**pahpeer
paperback	**ein Taschenbuch**	ighn **tah**shernbookh
paper napkins	**Papierservietten**	pahpeerzehrviehtern
paste	**Klebstoff**	**klaybshtof**
pen	**eine Feder**	**igh**ner **fay**derr
pencil	**einen Bleistift**	**igh**nern **bligh**shtift
pencil sharpener	**einen Bleistift-spitzer**	**igh**nern **bligh**shtiftshpitserr
playing cards	**Spielkarten**	**shpeel**kahrtern
postcards	**Postkarten**	**post**kahrtern
rubber	**einen Radiergummi**	**igh**nern rah**deer**gummi
ruler	**ein Lineal**	ighn linneh**arl**
sketching pad	**einen Zeichenblock**	**igh**nern **tsigh**khernblok
string	**Bindfaden/Schnur**	**bint**fardern/shnoor
thumbtacks	**Reißzwecken**	**righs**tsvehkern
tissue paper	**Seidenpapier**	**zigh**dernpahpeer
tracing paper	**Pauspapier**	**pows**pahpeer
typewriter ribbon	**ein Farbband**	ighn **fahrp**bahnt
typing paper	**Schreibmaschinen-papier**	**shrighp**mahsheenern-pahpeer
writing pad	**einen Schreibblock**	**igh**nern **shrighp**blok
Where's the guide-book section?	**Wo stehen die Reiseführer?**	voa **shtay**ern dee **righ**zerfewrerr
Where do you keep the English books?	**Wo stehen die englischen Bücher?**	voa **shtay**ern dee **ehng**lishern **bew**kherr
Have you any of...'s books in English?	**Haben Sie ein Buch von...in Englisch?**	**har**bern zee ighn bookh fon ... in **ehng**lish

Here are some contemporary German authors whose books are available in English translation:

Ingeborg Bachmann (Austrian)
Heinrich Böll
Friedrich Dürrenmatt (Swiss)
Max Frisch (Swiss)
Günter Grass
Uwe Johnson
Ernst Jünger
Siegfried Lenz
Martin Walser
Carl Zuckmayer

Camping

Here we're concerned with the equipment you may need.

I'd like a/an/some...	**Ich möchte...**	ikh **murkh**ter
axe	**eine Axt**	**igh**ner ahkst
bottle-opener	**einen Flaschenöffner**	**igh**nern **flah**shernurfnerr
bucket	**einen Eimer**	**igh**nern **igh**merr
butane gas	**Butangas**	but**tarn**gahss
camp bed	**ein Feldbett**	ighn **fehlt**beht
camping equipment	**eine Campingausrüstung**	**igh**ner **kehm**pingowsrewstung
can opener	**einen Büchsenöffner**	**igh**nern **bewk**sernurfnerr
candles	**Kerzen**	**kehr**tsern
chair	**einen Stuhl**	**igh**nern shtool
folding chair	**Klappstuhl**	**klahp**shtool
compass	**einen Kompaß**	**igh**nern **kom**pahss
corkscrew	**einen Korkenzieher**	**igh**nern **kor**kerntseeherr
crockery	**Geschirr**	ger**sheer**
cutlery	**Besteck**	ber**shtehk**
deck-chair	**einen Liegestuhl**	**igh**nern **lee**gershtool
first-aid kit	**einen Verbandkasten**	**igh**nern fehr**bahnt**kahstern
fishing tackle	**Angelzeug**	**ahng**erltsoyg
flashlight	**eine Taschenlampe**	**igh**ner **tah**shernlahmper
frying-pan	**eine Bratpfanne**	**igh**ner **brart**pfahner
groundsheet	**einen Zeltboden**	**igh**nern **tsehlt**boadern
hammer	**einen Hammer**	**igh**nern **hah**merr
hammock	**eine Hängematte**	**igh**ner **hehng**ermahter
haversack	**eine Provianttasche**	**igh**ner proavi**ahnt**tahsher
ice-bag	**einen Eisbehälter**	**igh**nern **ighs**berhehlterr
kerosene	**Petroleum**	pay**troa**layum
kettle	**einen Kessel**	**igh**nern **keh**sserl
knapsack	**einen Tornister**	**igh**nern tornisterr
lamp	**eine Lampe**	**igh**ner **lahm**per
lantern	**eine Laterne**	**igh**ner lah**tehr**ner
matches	**Streichhölzer**	**shtrighkh**hurltserr
mattress	**eine Matratze**	**igh**ner mah**trah**tser
methylated spirits	**Brennspiritus**	**brehn**shpeerittuss
pail	**einen Eimer**	**igh**nern **igh**merr
paraffin	**Petroleum**	pay**troa**layum
penknife	**ein Taschenmesser**	ighn **tah**shernmehsserr
picnic case	**einen Picknickkoffer**	**igh**nern **pik**nik-kofferr
pressure cooker	**einen Dampfkochtopf**	**igh**nern **dahmpf**kokhtopf
primus stove	**einen Primuskocher**	**igh**nern **pree**muskokherr
rope	**ein Seil**	ighn zighl

SHOPPING GUIDE

rucksack	**einen Rucksack**	ighnern **ruk**zahk
saucepan	**einen Kochtopf**	ighnern **kokh**topf
scissors	**eine Schere**	ighner **shay**rer
screwdriver	**einen Schrauben-zieher**	ighnern **shrow**berntseeherr
sheathknife	**ein Fahrtenmesser**	ighn **farr**ternmehsserr
sleeping bag	**einen Schlafsack**	ighnern **shlarf**zahk
stewpan	**einen Schmortopf**	ighnern **shmoar**topf
stove	**einen Kocher**	ighnern **ko**kherr
table	**einen Tisch**	ighnern tish
folding table	**Klapptisch**	**klahp**tish
tent	**ein Zelt**	ighn tsehlt
tent-pegs	**Heringe**	**hay**ringer
tent-pole	**eine Zeltstange**	ighner **tsehlt**shtahnger
thermos flask (bottle)	**eine Thermosflasche**	ighner **tehr**mosflahsher
tin-opener	**einen Büchsenöffner**	ighnern **bewk**sernurfnerr
tongs	**eine Zange**	ighner **tsahng**er
tool kit	**einen Werkzeug-kasten**	ighnern **vehrk**tsoygkahstern
torch	**eine Taschenlampe**	ighner **tah**shernlahmper
water carrier	**einen Wasser-kanister**	ighnern **vah**sserrkahnisterr
wood alcohol	**Brennspiritus**	**brehn**shpeerittuss

Crockery

cups	**die Tassen**	dee **tah**ssern
food box	**die Proviantkiste**	dee proa**viahnt**kister
mugs	**die Becher**	dee **beh**kherr
plates	**die Teller**	dee **teh**lerr
saucers	**die Untertassen**	dee **un**terrtahssern

Cutlery

forks	**die Gabeln**	dee **gar**berln
knives	**die Messer**	dee **meh**sserr
dessert knives	**die Dessertmesser**	dee deh**ssayr**mehsserr
spoons	**die Löffel**	dee **lur**ferl
teaspoons	**die Teelöffel**	dee **tay**lurferl
(made of) plastic	**(aus) Plastik**	(owss) **plah**stik
(made of) stainless steel	**(aus) rostfreiem Stahl**	(owss) **rost**frigherm shtarl

SHOPPING GUIDE

Chemist's—Drugstore

In German, a chemist's (drugstore) is called *Apotheke* (ahpo**tay**ker). These don't sell cameras, books and the like. If you're looking for toiletries, household articles or film, try a *Drogerie* (drogeh**ree**). You'll also find non-prescription medicine available in a *Drogerie.*

This section has been divided into two parts:

1. Pharmaceutical—medicine, first-aid, etc.
2. Toiletry—toilet articles, cosmetics

General

Where's the nearest (all-night) chemist's?	**Wo ist die nächste Apotheke (mit Nachtdienst)?**	voa ist dee **nehkh**ster ahpoa**tay**ker (mit **nahkht**deenst)
What time does the chemist's open/close?	**Um wieviel Uhr öffnet/schließt die Apotheke?**	um **vee**feel oor **urf**nert/shleest dee ahpoa**tay**ker

Part 1—Pharmaceutical

I want something for...	**Ich möchte etwas gegen...**	ikh **murkh**ter **eht**vahss **gay**gern
a cold	**eine Erkältung**	**igh**ner ehr**kehl**tung
a cough	**Husten**	**hoo**stern
a hangover	**Kater**	**kar**terr
hay fever	**Heuschnupfen**	**hoy**shnupfern
sunburn	**Sonnenbrand**	**son**nenbrahnt
travel sickness	**Reisekrankheit**	**righ**zerkrahnk-hight
an upset stomach	**Magenverstimmung**	**mar**gernfehrshtimmung
Can you make up this prescription for me?	**Können Sie mir dieses Rezept machen?**	**kur**nern zee meer **dee**zerss reh**tsehpt** **mah**khern
Shall I wait?	**Soll ich warten?**	zol ikh **vahr**tern
When shall I come back?	**Wann kann ich zurückkommen?**	vahn kahn ikh tsoo**rewk**kommern
Can I get it without a prescription?	**Kann ich das ohne Rezept bekommen?**	kahn ikh dahss **oa**ner reh**tsehpt** ber**kom**mern

FOR DOCTOR, see page 162

Can I have a/an/ some...?	**Kann ich... haben?**	kahn ikh... **har**bern
ammonia	**Ammoniak**	ahmonni**ahk**
antiseptic cream	**eine Wundsalbe**	**igh**ner **vunt**zahlber
aspirin	**Aspirin**	ahspee**reen**
bandage	**einen Verband**	**igh**nern fehr**bahnt**
crepe bandage	**eine elastische Binde**	**igh**ner eh**lahs**tisher **bin**der
gauze bandage	**eine Mullbinde**	**igh**ner **mul**binder
Band-Aids	**Heftpflaster**	**hehft**pflahsterr
calcium tablets	**Kalktabletten**	**kahlk**tahblehtern
castor oil	**Rizinusöl**	**rit**sinnussurl
chlorine tablets	**Chlortabletten**	**kloar**tahblehtern
contraceptive	**ein Verhütungsmittel**	ighn fehr**hew**tungsmitterl
corn plasters	**Hühneraugenpflaster**	**hew**nerrowgernpflahsterr
cotton wool	**Watte**	**vah**ter
cough drops	**Hustenbonbons**	**hoo**sternbongbong
diabetic lozenges	**Diabetikerpastillen**	diah**bay**tikkerpahstillern
disinfectant	**ein Desinfektionsmittel**	ighn dehsinfehk**tsioans**mitterl
ear drops	**Ohrentropfen**	**oa**rerntropfern
Elastoplast	**Heftpflaster**	**hehft**pflahsterr
eye drops	**Augentropfen**	**ow**gerntropfern
first-aid kit	**einen Verbandkasten**	**igh**nern fehr**bahnt**kahstern
gargle	**Gurgelwasser**	**goor**gerlvahsserr
gauze	**Verbandmull**	fehr**bahnt**mul
insect lotion	**ein Insektenmittel**	ighn in**zehk**ternmitterl
iodine	**Jod**	yoat
iron pills	**Eisentabletten**	**igh**zerntahblehtern
laxative	**ein Abführmittel**	ighn **ahp**fewrmitterl
lint	**Verbandmull**	fehr**bahnt**mul
mouthwash	**Mundwasser**	**munt**vahsserr
sanitary napkins	**Damenbinden**	**dar**mernbindern
sedative	**ein Beruhigungsmittel**	ighn ber**roo**igungsmitterl
sleeping pills	**Schlaftabletten**	**shlarf**tahblehtern
stomach pills	**Magentabletten**	**mar**gerntahblehtern
thermometer	**ein Thermometer**	ighn thermom**may**terr
throat lozenges	**Halspastillen**	**hahls**pahstillern
tonic	**ein Stärkungsmittel**	ighn **shtehr**kungsmitterl
vitamin pills	**Vitamintabletten**	vittah**meen**tahblehtern
weight-reducing tablets	**Schlankheitspillen**	**shlahngk**hightspillern

Part 2—Toiletry

I'd like a/an some...	**Ich hätte gerne...**	ikh **heh**ter **gehr**ner
acne cream	**eine Aknesalbe**	**igh**ner **ahk**nerzahlber
after-shave lotion	**ein Rasierwasser**	ighn rah**zeer**vahsserr
astringent	**ein Adstringens**	ighn ahd**stringe**hns
bath essence	**Badeessenz**	**bar**derehssehnts
bath salts	**Badesalz**	**bar**derzahlts
cologne	**ein Kölnischwasser**	ighn kurlnish**vah**sserr
cream	**eine Creme**	**igh**ner kraym
cleansing cream	**Reinigungscreme**	**righ**niggungskraym
cuticle cream	**Nagelhautcreme**	**nar**gerlhowtkraym
enzyme cream	**Enzymcreme**	ehn**tsewm**kraym
hormone cream	**Hormoncreme**	hor**moan**kraym
moisturizing cream	**Feuchtigkeitscreme**	**foykh**tikhkightskraym
night cream	**Nachtcreme**	**nahkht**kraym
cuticle remover	**Nagelhautentferner**	**nar**gerlhowtehntfehrnerr
deodorant	**ein Desodorans**	ighn dehzoadoa**rahns**
emery board	**eine Sandpapierfeile**	**igh**ner **zahnt**pahpeerfighler
eye liner	**einen Lidstift**	**igh**nern **leed**shtift
eye pencil	**einen Augenbrauen-stift**	**igh**nern **ow**gernbrowern-shtift
eye shadow	**einen Lidschatten**	**igh**nern **leed**shahtern
face pack	**eine Gesichtsmaske**	**igh**ner ger**zikhts**mahsker
face powder	**Gesichtspuder**	ger**zikhts**pooderr
foot cream	**Fußcreme**	**foos**kraym
foot powder	**Fußpuder**	**foos**pooderr
hand cream	**Handcreme**	**hahnt**kraym
hand lotion	**Handlotion**	**hahnt**lotsioan
lipsalve	**eine Lippenpomade**	**igh**ner **lip**pernpommarder
lipstick	**einen Lippenstift**	**igh**nern **lip**pernshtift
lipstick brush	**einen Lippenpinsel**	**igh**nern **lip**pernpinzerl
make-up bag	**einen Kosmetik-beutel**	**igh**nern kos**may**tikboyterl
make-up remover pads	**Abschminkwatte**	**ahp**shmingkvahter
mascara	**Wimperntusche**	**vim**perrntusher
nail brush	**eine Nagelbürste**	**igh**ner **nar**gerlbewrster
nail clippers	**eine Nagelzange**	**igh**ner **nar**gerltsahnger
nail file	**eine Nagelfeile**	**igh**ner **nar**gerlfighler
nail polish	**Nagellack**	**nar**gerllahk
nail polish remover	**Nagellackentferner**	**nar**gerllahkehntfehrnerr
nail scissors	**eine Nagelschere**	**igh**ner **nar**gerlshayrer
perfume	**ein Parfüm**	ighn pahr**fewm**
powder	**Puder**	**poo**derr
pumice stone	**einen Bimsstein**	**igh**nern **bims**shtighn
razor	**einen Rasierapparat**	**igh**nern rah**zeer**ahpahrart

SHOPPING GUIDE

razor blades	**Rasierklingen**	rah**zeer**klingern
rouge	**Rouge**	roozh
safety pins	**Sicherheitsnadeln**	**zi**kherrhightsnarderln
shampoo	**ein Haarwaschmittel**	ighn **harr**vahshmitterl
shaving brush	**einen Rasierpinsel**	**igh**nern rah**zeer**pinzerl
shaving cream	**Rasiercreme**	rah**zeer**kraym
shaving soap	**Rasierseife**	rah**zeer**zighfer
soap	**eine Seife**	**igh**ner **zigh**fer
sponge	**einen Schwamm**	**igh**nern shvahm
sun-tan cream	**Sonnencreme**	**son**nernkraym
sun-tan oil	**Sonnenöl**	**son**nernurl
talcum powder	**Talkumpuder**	**tahl**kumpooderr
tissues	**Papiertücher**	pah**peer**tewkherr
toilet paper	**Toilettenpapier**	toaah**leh**ternpahpeer
toilet water	**ein Toilettenwasser**	ighn toaah**leh**ternvahsserr
toothbrush	**eine Zahnbürste**	**igh**ner **tsarn**bewrster
toothpaste	**Zahnpasta**	**tsarn**pahstar
toothpowder	**Zahnpuder**	**tsarn**pooderr
tweezers	**eine Pinzette**	**igh**ner pint**seh**ter

For your hair

bobby pins	**Haarklemmen**	**harr**klehmern
brush	**eine Haarbürste**	**igh**ner **harr**bewrster
comb	**einen Kamm**	**igh**nern kahm
dye	**ein Färbemittel**	ighn **fehr**bermitterl
grips	**Haarklips**	**harr**klips
lacquer	**einen Haarlack**	**igh**nern **harr**lahk
oil	**ein Haaröl**	ighn **harr**url
pins	**Haarnadeln**	**harr**narderln
rollers	**Lockenwickler**	**lok**kernviklerr
setting lotion	**einen Haarfestiger**	**igh**nern **harr**fehstigerr
tint	**ein Tönungsmittel**	ighn **tur**nungsmitterl

For the baby

bib	**ein Lätzchen**	ighn **lehts**khern
diapers (nappies)	**Windeln**	**vin**derln
diaper pins	**Windelklammern**	**vin**derlklahmerrn
dummy (pacifier)	**einen Schnuller**	**igh**nern **shnul**lerr
plastic pants	**ein Plastikhöschen**	ighn **plah**stikhurskhern

Clothing

If you want to buy something specific, prepare yourself in advance. Look at the list of clothing on page 117. Get some idea of the colour, material and size you want. They're all listed on the next few pages.

General

I'd like...	**Ich möchte...**	ikh **murkh**ter
I want...for a 10-year-old boy.	**Ich möchte...für einen 10-jährigen Jungen.**	ikh **murkh**ter ... fewr **igh**nern 10-**yai**riggern **yun**gern
I want something like this.	**Ich möchte etwas in dieser Art.**	ikh **murkh**ter **eht**vahss in **dee**zerr arrt
I like the one in the window.	**Das im Schaufenster gefällt mir.**	dahss im **show**fehnsterr ger**fehlt** meer
How much is that per metre?	**Wieviel kostet der Meter?**	vee**feel kos**tert derr **may**terr

1 centimetre = 0.39 in.	1 inch = 2.54 cm.
1 metre = 39.37 in.	1 foot = 30.5 cm.
10 metres = 32.81 ft.	1 yard = 0.91 m.

Colour

I want something in...	**Ich möchte etwas in...**	ikh **murkh**ter **eht**vahss in
I want a darker shade.	**Ich möchte es etwas dunkler.**	ikh **murkh**ter ehss **eht**vahss **dungk**lerr
I want something to match this.	**Ich möchte etwas hierzu Passendes.**	ikh **murkh**ter **eht**vahss **heer**tsoo **pah**ssernderss
I don't like the colour.	**Die Farbe gefällt mir nicht.**	dee **fahr**ber ger**fehlt** meer nikht

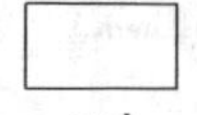

uni
(unni)

gestreift
(ger**shtrighft**)

gepunktet
(ger**pungk**tert)

kariert
(kah**reert**)

gemustert
(ger**mus**terrt)

beige	**beige**	bayzh
black	**schwarz**	shvahrts
blue	**blau**	blow
brown	**braun**	brown
cream	**creme**	kraym
crimson	**karmin-rot**	kahr**meen** roat
emerald	**smaragdgrün**	smah**rahgt**grewn
fawn	**hellbraun**	**hehl**brown
gold	**golden**	**gol**dern
green	**grün**	grewn
grey	**grau**	grow
mauve	**lila**	**lee**lah
orange	**orangenfarben**	oa**rahng**zhernfahrbern
pink	**rosa**	**roa**zah
purple	**purpurrot**	**poor**poorroat
red	**rot**	roat
scarlet	**scharlachrot**	**shahr**lahkhroat
silver	**silbern**	**zil**berrn
tan	**bräunlich**	**broyn**likh
turquoise	**türkisfarben**	tewr**kees**fahrbern
white	**weiß**	vighss
yellow	**gelb**	gehlp

Material

Do you have anything in...?	**Haben Sie etwas in...?**	**har**bern zee **eht**vahss in
I want a cotton blouse.	**Ich möchte eine Baumwollbluse.**	ikh **murkh**ter **igh**ner **bowm**volbloozer
Is that...?	**Ist das...?**	ist dahss
hand-made	**Handarbeit**	**hahnt**ahrbight
imported	**importiert**	impor**teert**
made here	**inländisches Fabrikat**	**in**lehndisherss fahbrik**kart**
I want something thinner.	**Ich möchte etwas Dünneres.**	ikh **murkh**ter **eht**vahss **dew**nerrerss
Do you have any better quality?	**Haben Sie eine bessere Qualität?**	**har**bern zee **igh**ner **beh**sserrer kvahli**tait**
What's it made of?	**Welches Material ist das?**	**vehl**kherss mahteh**riarl** ist dahss

It may be made of…

cambric	**Batist**	bah**tist**
camel-hair	**Kamelhaar**	kah**mayl**harr
chiffon	**Chiffon**	shif**foan**
corduroy	**Kord**	kort
cotton	**Baumwolle**	**bowm**voller
crepe	**Krepp**	krehp
denim	**Drillich**	**dril**likh
felt	**Filz**	filts
flannel	**Flanell**	flah**nehl**
gabardine	**Gabardine**	**gah**bahrdin
lace	**Spitze**	**shpi**tser
leather	**Leder**	**lay**derr
linen	**Leinen**	**ligh**nern
needlecord	**Feinkord**	**fighn**kort
piqué	**Pikee**	pik**kay**
poplin	**Popeline**	popper**leen**
rayon	**Kunstseide**	**kunst**sighder
satin	**Satin**	sah**tehng**
silk	**Seide**	**zigh**der
suede	**Wildleder**	**vilt**layderr
taffeta	**Taft**	tahft
terrycloth	**Frottee**	frot**tay**
tulle	**Tüll**	tewl
tweed	**Tweed**	tveet
velvet	**Samt**	zahmt
veveteen	**Manchester**	mahn**sheh**sterr
velour	**Velours**	veh**loor**
wool	**Wolle**	**vol**ler
worsted	**Kammgarn**	**kahm**gahrn
synthetic	**synthetisch**	zewn**tay**tish
wash and wear	**bügelfrei**	**bew**gerlfrigh
wrinkle-resistant	**knitterfrei**	**knit**terrfrigh

Size

My size is 38.	**Ich habe Größe 38.**	ikh **har**ber **grur**sser 38
I don't know your sizes. Could you measure me?	**Ich kenne Ihre Größen nicht. Können Sie mir Maß nehmen?**	ikh **keh**ner **ee**rer **grur**ssern nikht. **kur**nern zee meer mahss **nay**mern

If you don't know continental sizes, consult the charts on the next page.

This is your size

In Europe as in Britain and the U.S., sizes vary somewhat from country to country. These charts should therefore be considered as an approximate guide.

Ladies

Dresses/Suits						
American	10	12	14	16	18	20
British	32	34	36	38	40	42
Continental	38	40	42	44	46	48

Stockings						
American / British	8	8½	9	9½	10	10½
Continental	0	1	2	3	4	5

Shoes				
American	6	7	8	9
British	4½	5½	6½	7½
Continental	37	38	40	41

Gentlemen

Suits/Overcoats						
American / British	36	38	40	42	44	46
Continental	46	48	50	52	54	56

Shirts				
American / British	15	16	17	18
Continental	38	41	43	45

Shoes									
American / British	5	6	7	8	8½	9	9½	10	11
Continental	38	39	41	42	43	43	44	44	45

A good fit?

Can I try it on?	**Kann ich es anprobieren?**	kahn ikh ehss **ahn**proabeerern
Where's the fitting room?	**Wo ist die Umkleidekabine?**	voa ist dee **um**klighderkahbeener
Is there a mirror?	**Hat es einen Spiegel?**	haht ehss **igh**nern **shpee**gerl
Does it fit?	**Paßt es?**	pahst ehss

FOR NUMBERS, see page 175

It fits very well.	**Es paßt ausgezeichnet.**	ehss pahst **ows**ger-tsighkhnert
It doesn't fit.	**Es paßt nicht.**	ehss pahst nikht
It's too...	**Es ist zu...**	ehss ist tsu
short/long tight/loose	**kurz/lang eng/weit**	koorts/lahng ehng/vight
How long will it take to alter?	**Wie lange brauchen Sie, um es zu ändern?**	vee **lah**nger **brow**khern zee um ehss tsu **ehn**derrn

Shoes

I'd like a pair of...	**Ich möchte ein Paar...**	ikh **murkh**ter ighn parr
shoes/sandals boots/slippers	**Schuhe/Sandalen Stiefel/Hausschuhe**	**shoo**er/zahn**dar**lern **shtee**ferl/**hows**shooer
These are too...	**Diese sind zu...**	**dee**zer zint tsu
narrow/wide large/small	**eng/weit groß/klein**	ehng/vight groass/klighn
They pinch my toes.	**Sie drücken an den Zehen.**	zee **drew**kern ahn dayn **tsay**ern
Do you have a larger size?	**Haben Sie eine größere Nummer?**	**har**bern zee **igh**ner **grurs**serrer **num**merr
I want a smaller size.	**Ich möchte eine kleinere Nummer.**	ikh **murkh**ter **igh**ner **kligh**nerrer **num**merr
Do you have the same in...?	**Haben Sie die gleichen in...?**	**har**bern zee dee **gligh**khern in
brown/beige black/white	**braun/beige schwarz/weiß**	brown/bayzh shvahrts/vighss

Shoes worn out? Here's the key to getting them fixed again:

Can you repair these shoes?	**Können Sie diese Schuhe reparieren?**	**kur**nern zee **dee**zer **shoo**er rehpah**ree**rern
Can you stitch this?	**Können Sie das nähen?**	**kur**nern zee dahss **nai**ern
I want new soles and heels.	**Ich möchte neue Sohlen und Absätze.**	ikh **murkh**ter **noy**er **zoa**lern unt **ahp**zehtser
When will they be ready?	**Wann sind sie fertig?**	vahn zint zee **fehr**tikh

Clothes and accessories

I'd like a/an/some...	**Ich hätte gerne...**	ikh **heh**ter **gehr**ner
anorak	**einen Anorak**	**igh**nern **ahn**orrahk
bath robe	**einen Bademantel**	**igh**nern **bar**dermahnterl
blazer	**einen Blazer**	**igh**nern **blay**zerr
blouse	**eine Bluse**	**igh**ner **bloo**zer
bow tie	**eine Fliege**	**igh**ner **flee**ger
bra	**einen Büstenhalter**	**igh**nern **bew**sternhahlterr
braces	**Hosenträger**	**hoa**zerntraigerr
briefs	**eine kurze Unterhose**	**igh**ner **koort**ser **un**terrhoazer
cap	**eine Mütze**	**igh**ner **mewt**ser
cardigan	**eine Wollweste**	**igh**ner **vol**vehster
coat	**einen Mantel**	**igh**nern **mahn**terl
dinner jacket	**einen Smoking**	**igh**nern **smoa**king
dress	**ein Kleid**	ighn klight
dressing gown	**einen Morgenrock**	**igh**nern **mor**gernrok
evening dress	**ein Abendkleid**	ighn **ar**berntklight
frock	**ein Kleid**	ighn klight
fur coat	**einen Pelzmantel**	**igh**nern **pehlts**mahnterl
garter belt	**einen Strumpfgürtel**	**igh**nern **shtrumpf**gewrterl
girdle	**einen Hüfthalter**	**igh**nern **hewft**hahlterr
gloves	**Handschuhe**	**hahnt**shooer
gym shoes	**Turnschuhe**	**toorn**shooer
handkerchief	**ein Taschentuch**	ighn **tah**sherntookh
hat	**einen Hut**	**igh**nern hoot
housecoat	**einen Hausmantel**	**igh**nern **hows**mahnterl
jacket	**ein Jackett/eine Jacke**	ighn zhah**keht/igh**ner **yah**ker
jeans	**Jeans**	"jeans"
jersey	**eine Strickjacke**	**igh**ner **shtrik**yahker
jumper (Br.)	**einen Pullover**	**igh**nern pul**loa**verr
jumper (Am.)	**einen Trägerrock**	**igh**nern **trai**gerrrok
leather trousers	**eine Lederhose**	**igh**ner **lay**derrhoazer
lingerie	**Unterwäsche**	**un**terrvehsher
mackintosh	**einen Regenmantel**	**igh**nern **ray**gernmahnterl
negligé	**ein Negligé**	ighn nehgli**zhay**
nightdress	**ein Nachthemd**	ighn **nahkht**hehmt
overcoat	**einen Mantel**	**igh**nern **mahn**terl
pair of...	**ein Paar...**	ighn parr
panties	**einen Schlüpfer**	**igh**nern **shlew**pferr
pants	**eine Hose**	**igh**ner **hoa**zer
pants suit	**einen Hosenanzug**	**igh**nern **hoa**zernahntsoog
panty-girdle	**ein Strumpfhalterhöschen**	ighn **shtrumpf**hahlterr-hurskhern

SHOPPING GUIDE

panty hose	**eine Strumpfhose**	igh**ner shtrumpf**hoazer
parka	**einen Anorak**	igh**nern ahnoarahk**
pullover	**einen Pullover**	igh**nern pull**o**averr**
pyjamas	**einen Schlafanzug**	igh**nern shlarf**ahntsoog
raincoat	**einen Regenmantel**	igh**nern raygernmahnterl**
scarf	**ein Halstuch**	ighn **hahls**tookh
shirt	**ein Hemd**	ighn hehmt
shoes	**Schuhe**	shooer
shorts	**Shorts**	"shorts"
skirt	**einen Rock**	igh**nern rok**
slip	**einen Unterrock**	igh**nern unterrok**
slippers	**Hausschuhe**	**howsshooer**
socks	**Socken**	**zok**kern
sports jacket	**eine Sportjacke**	igh**ner shport**yahker
stockings	**Strümpfe**	**shtrewm**pfer
suit (man's)	**einen Anzug**	igh**nern ahntsoog**
suit (woman's)	**ein Kostüm**	ighn **kostewm**
suspender belt	**einen Strumpfgürtel**	igh**nern shtrumpf**gewrterl
suspenders (Am.)	**Hosenträger**	**hoazerntraigerr**
sweater	**einen Pullover**	igh**nern pull**o**averr**
swimsuit	**einen Badeanzug**	igh**nern barderahntsoog**
T-shirt	**ein T-Shirt**	ighn "T-shirt"
tennis shoes	**Tennisschuhe**	**tehnisshooer**
tie	**eine Krawatte**	igh**ner krah**v**ahter**
top coat	**einen Überzieher**	igh**nern ewberrtseeherr**
track suit	**einen Trainings-anzug**	igh**nern trainingsahntsoog**
trousers	**eine Hose**	igh**ner hoazer**
underpants (men)	**eine Unterhose**	igh**ner unterrhoazer**
undershirt	**ein Unterhemd**	ighn **unterrhehmt**
vest (Am.)	**eine Weste**	igh**ner vehster**
vest (Br.)	**ein Unterhemd**	ighn **unterrhehmt**
waistcoat	**eine Weste**	igh**ner vehster**

belt	**der Gürtel**	derr **gewrterl**
buckle	**die Schnalle**	dee **shnahler**
button	**der Knopf**	derr knopf
collar	**der Kragen**	derr **krargern**
cuffs	**die Manschetten**	dee mahn**shehtern**
elastic	**das Gummiband**	dahss **gummibahnt**
pocket	**die Tasche**	dee **tahsher**
shoe laces	**die Schnürsenkel**	dee **shnewr**zehnkerl
sleeve	**der Ärmel**	derr **airmerl**
zip (zipper)	**der Reißverschluß**	derr **righs**fehrshluss

Electrical appliances and accessories—Records

220 volts, 50-cycle AC is almost universal in Germany as well as in Austria and Switzerland. Nevertheless, check the voltage before you plug your appliance in. You'll find an adaptor useful since the round pins on continental plugs are different from ours.

What's the voltage?	**Welche Spannung haben Sie hier?**	**vehl**kher **shpah**nung **har**bern zee heer
Is it AC or DC?	**Ist es Wechselstrom oder Gleichstrom?**	ist ehss **vehk**serlshtroam oaderr **glighkh**shtroam
Do you have a battery for...?	**Haben Sie eine Batterie für...?**	**har**bern zee **igh**ner bahteh**ree** fewr
Can you repair that?	**Können Sie das reparieren?**	**kur**nern zee dahss rehpah**ree**rern
When will it be ready?	**Wann ist es fertig?**	vahn ist ehss **fehr**tikh
I'd like a/an/some...	**Ich möchte...**	ikh **murkh**ter
adaptor	**einen Zwischenstecker**	**igh**nern **tsvi**shernshtehkerr
amplifier	**einen Verstärker**	**igh**nern fehr**shtair**kerr
battery	**eine Batterie**	**igh**ner bahteh**ree**
blender	**einen Mixer**	**igh**nern **mik**serr
clock	**eine Uhr**	**igh**ner oor
wall clock	**Wanduhr**	**vahnt**oor
food mixer	**einen Stabmixer**	**igh**nern **shtarp**mikserr
hair dryer	**einen Haartrockner**	**igh**nern **harr**troknerr
iron	**ein Bügeleisen**	ighn **bew**gerlighzern
travelling iron	**Reisebügeleisen**	**righ**zerbewgerlighzern
kettle	**einen Wassertopf**	**igh**nern **vah**sserrtopf
percolator	**eine Kaffeemaschine**	**igh**ner **kah**faymahsheener
plug	**einen Stecker**	**igh**nern **shteh**kerr
portable	**Koffer...**	**kof**ferr
radio	**ein Radio**	ighn **rar**dioa
car radio	**Autoradio**	**ow**toarardioa
record player	**einen Plattenspieler**	**igh**nern **plah**ternshpeelerr
shaver	**einen Rasierapparat**	**igh**nern rah**zeer**ahpahrart
speakers	**Lautsprecher**	**lowt**shprehkherr
tape recorder	**ein Tonbandgerät**	ighn **toan**bahntgerrait
cassette tape recorder	**einen Kassettenrekorder**	**igh**nern kah**sseh**ternrehkorderr

television	**einen Fernseher**	igh nern **fehrn**zayerr
colour television	**Farbfernseher**	**fahrp**fehrnzayerr
toaster	**einen Toaster**	**igh**nern **toaster**
transformer	**einen Transformator**	**igh**nern trahnsfor**mar**toar

Record shop

Do you have any records by...?	**Haben Sie Platten von...?**	**har**bern zee **plah**tern fon
Do you have...'s latest album?	**Haben Sie das neuste Album von...?**	**har**bern zee dahss **noy**ster **ahl**bum fon
Can I listen to this record?	**Kann ich diese Platte hören?**	kahn ikh **dee**zer **plah**ter **hur**rern
I'd like a cassette.	**Ich hätte gern eine Kassette.**	ikh **heh**ter gehrn **igh**ner kahs**seh**ter
I want a new needle.	**Ich möchte eine neue Nadel.**	ikh **murkh**ter **igh**ner **noy**er **nar**derl

L.P.	**die Langspielplatte**	dee **lahng**shpeelplahter
45 rpm	**fünfundvierzig UpM**	**fewn**funtfeertsikh oo pay ehm
33 rpm	**dreiunddreißig UpM**	**drigh**untdrighssikh oo pay ehm

chamber music	**die Kammermusik**	dee **kah**merrmuzeek
classical music	**die klassische Musik**	dee **klah**ssisher mu**zeek**
folk music	**die Volksmusik**	dee **folks**muzeek
instrumental music	**die Instrumentalmusik**	dee instrumehn**tarl**muzeek
jazz	**der Jazz**	derr dzhaiss
light music	**die Unterhaltungsmusik**	dee unterr**hahl**tungsmuzeek
orchestral music	**die Orchestermusik**	dee or**keh**sterrmuzeek
pop music	**die Pop-Musik**	dee **pop**muzeek
yodelling music	**die Jodelmusik**	dee **yoa**derlmuzeek

Here are the names of a few popular recording artists:

Peter Alexander
Katja Ebstein
Gitte
Heino
Udo Jürgens
Hildegard Knef
Jürgen Marcus
Reinhard Mey
Monica Morell
Mary Roos

Hairdressing—Barber's

I don't speak much German.	**Ich spreche nicht viel Deutsch.**	ikh **shprehk**her nikht feel doych
I want a haircut, please.	**Haare schneiden, bitte.**	harrer **shnigh**dern **bit**ter
I'd like a shave.	**Rasieren, bitte.**	rahzeerern **bit**ter
Don't cut it too short.	**Nicht zu kurz.**	nikht tsu **koorts**
Scissors only, please.	**Nur mit der Schere, bitte.**	noor mit derr **shay**rer **bit**ter
A razor cut, please.	**Einen Messer-schnitt, bitte.**	**igh**nern **meh**sserrshnit **bit**ter
Don't use the clippers.	**Bitte keine Maschine.**	**bit**ter **kigh**ner mah**shee**ner
Just a trim, please.	**Nur ausputzen, bitte.**	noor **ow**sputsern **bit**ter
That's enough off.	**Das genügt.**	dahss ger**newgt**
A little more off the...	**Nehmen Sie...ein bißchen mehr weg.**	**nay**mern zee ... ighn **bis**khern mayr vehk
back	**hinten**	**hin**tern
neck	**im Nacken**	im **nah**kern
sides	**an den Seiten**	ahn dayn **zigh**tern
top	**oben**	**oa**bern
I don't want any cream.	**Ich möchte keine Creme.**	ikh **murkh**ter **kigh**ner kraym
Would you please trim my...?	**Stutzen Sie mir bitte...**	**shtut**sern zee meer **bit**ter
beard	**den Bart**	dayn barrt
moustache	**den Schnurrbart**	dayn **shnoor**barrt
sideboards (sideburns)	**die Koteletten**	dee kot**leh**tern
Thank you. That's fine.	**Sehr gut, danke.**	zayr goot **dahng**ker
How much do I owe you?	**Was schulde ich Ihnen?**	vahss **shul**der ikh **ee**nern
This is for you.	**Das ist für Sie.**	dahss ist fewr zee

FOR TIPPING, see inside back-cover

SHOPPING GUIDE

Ladies' hairdressing

Is there a hairdresser's in the hotel?	**Gibt es einen Damensalon im Hotel?**	gipt ehss **igh**nern **dar**mernzahlong im hoa**tehl**
Can I make an appointment for sometime on Thursday?	**Kann ich mich für Donnerstag anmelden?**	kahn ikh mikh fewr **don**nerrstarg **ahn**mehldern
I'd like it cut and shaped.	**Schneiden und Legen, bitte.**	**shnigh**dern unt **lay**gern **bit**ter

with a fringe (bangs)	**Ponyfrisur**	poanifreezoor
page-boy style	**Pagenschnitt**	parzhernshnit
a razor cut	**ein Messerschnitt**	ighn **meh**sserrshnit
a re-style	**eine neue Frisur**	**igh**ner **noy**er free**zoor**
with ringlets	**mit Löckchen**	mit **lurk**khern
with waves	**mit Wellen**	mit **veh**lern
in a bun	**im Knoten**	im **knoa**tern

I want a...	**Bitte...**	**bit**ter
bleach	**eine Aufhellung**	**igh**ner **owf**hehlung
colour rinse	**eine Farbspülung**	**igh**ner **fahrp**shpewlung
dye	**eine Färbung**	**igh**ner **fair**bung
permanent	**eine Dauerwelle**	**igh**ner **dow**errvehler
shampoo and set	**Waschen und Legen**	**vah**shern unt **lay**gern
tint	**eine Tönung**	**igh**ner **tur**nung
touch up	**eine Auffrischung**	**igh**ner **owf**frishung
the same colour	**dieselbe Farbe**	dee**zehl**ber **fahr**ber
a darker colour	**eine dunklere Farbe**	**igh**ner **dungk**lerrer **fahr**ber
a lighter colour	**eine hellere Farbe**	**igh**ner **heh**lerrer **fahr**ber
auburn/blond/brunette	**kastanienbraun/blond/braun**	kah**star**niernbrown/blont/brown
Do you have a colour chart?	**Haben Sie eine Farbtabelle?**	**har**bern zee **igh**ner **fahrp**tahbehler
I don't want any hairspray.	**Kein Haarspray, bitte.**	kighn **harr**shpray **bit**ter
I want a...	**Ich möchte eine...**	ikh **murkh**ter **igh**ner
manicure/pedicure	**Maniküre/Pediküre**	**mah**nikkewrer/**peh**dikkewrer
face-pack	**Gesichtsmaske**	ger**zikhts**mahsker

FOR TIPPING, see inside back-cover

SHOPPING GUIDE

Jeweller's—Watchmaker's

Can you repair this watch?	**Können Sie diese Uhr reparieren?**	**kur**nern zee **dee**zer oor rehpah**ree**rern
The...is broken.	**...ist kaputt.**	...ist kah**put**
glass / spring	**das Glas/die Feder**	dahss glahss/dee **fay**derr
strap	**das Armband**	dahss **ahrm**bahnt
winder	**der Kronenaufzug**	derr **kroa**nernowftsoog
I want this watch cleaned.	**Ich möchte diese Uhr reinigen lassen.**	ikh **murkh**ter **dee**zer oor **righ**niggern **lah**ssern
When will it be ready?	**Wann ist sie fertig?**	vahn ist zee **fehr**tikh
Could I please see that?	**Könnte ich das bitte sehen?**	**kurn**ter ikh dahss **bit**ter **zay**ern
I'm just looking around.	**Ich sehe mich nur um.**	ikh **zay**er mikh noor um
I want a small present for...	**Ich möchte ein kleines Geschenk für...**	ikh **murkh**ter ighn **kligh**nerss ger**shehngk** fewr
I don't want anything too expensive.	**Ich möchte nichts zu Teures.**	ikh **murkh**ter nikhts tsu **toy**rerss
I want something...	**Ich möchte etwas...**	ikh **murkh**ter **eht**vahss
better/cheaper	**Besseres/Billigeres**	**beh**sserrerss/**bil**ligerrerss
simpler	**Einfacheres**	**ighn**fahkherrerss
Is this real silver?	**Ist das echt Silber?**	ist dahss ekht **zil**berr
Do you have anything in gold?	**Haben Sie etwas in Gold?**	**har**bern zee **eht**vahss in golt

If it's made of gold, ask:

How many carats is this?	**Wieviel Karat hat es?**	vee**feel** kah**rart** haht ehss

When you go to a jeweller's, you've probably got some idea of what you want beforehand. Find out what the article is made of and then look up the name of the article itself in the following lists.

What's it made of?

amber	**Bernstein**	**behrn**shtighn
amethyst	**Amethyst**	ahmeh**tist**
chromium	**Chrom**	kroam
copper	**Kupfer**	**kup**ferr
coral	**Koralle**	kor**rah**ler
crystal	**Kristall**	kris**tahl**
cut glass	**geschliffenes Glas**	ger**shlif**fernerss glahss
diamond	**Diamant**	diah**mahnt**
ebony	**Ebenholz**	**ay**bernholts
emerald	**Smaragd**	smah**rahgt**
enamel	**Email**	eh**mahi**
glass	**Glas**	glahss
gold	**Gold**	golt
gold plate	**vergoldet**	fehr**gol**dert
ivory	**Elfenbein**	**ehl**fernbighn
jade	**Jade**	yarder
onyx	**Onyx**	**oa**niks
pearl	**Perle**	**pehr**ler
pewter	**Zinn**	tsin
platinum	**Platin**	**plar**teen
ruby	**Rubin**	ru**been**
sapphire	**Saphir**	zah**feer**
silver	**Silber**	**zil**berr
silver plate	**versilbert**	fehr**zil**bert
stainless steel	**rostfreier Stahl**	**rost**frigherr shtarl
topaz	**Topas**	top**parss**
turquoise	**Türkis**	tewr**keess**

What is it?

I'd like a/an/some...	**Ich möchte...**	ikh **murkh**ter
bangle	**einen Reif**	**igh**nern righf
beads	**eine Perlenschnur**	**igh**ner **pehr**lernshnoor
bracelet	**ein Armband**	ighn **ahrm**bahnt
charm bracelet	**Amulettarmband**	ahmul**leht**ahrmbahnt
brooch	**eine Brosche**	**igh**ner **bro**sher
chain	**ein Kettchen**	ighn **keht**khern
charm	**ein Amulett**	ighn ahmul**leht**
cigarette case	**ein Zigarettenetui**	ighn tsiggah**reh**ternehtvee
cigarette lighter	**ein Feuerzeug**	ighn **foy**errtsoyg
clock	**eine Uhr**	**igh**ner oor
alarm clock	**einen Wecker**	**igh**nern **veh**kerr
cuckoo clock	**eine Kuckucksuhr**	**igh**ner **kuk**kuksoor

travelling clock	**einen Reisewecker**	**igh**nern **righ**zervehkerr
wall clock	**eine Wanduhr**	ighner **vahnd**oor
collar stud	**einen Kragenknopf**	**igh**nern **krar**gernknopf
cross	**ein Kreuz**	ighn kroyts
cuff-links	**Manschettenknöpfe**	mahn**sheh**ternknurpfer
earrings	**Ohrringe**	**oar**ringer
jewel box	**ein Schmuck-kästchen**	ighn **shmuk**-kehstkhern
manicure set	**ein Maniküreetui**	ighn mahnik**kewr**ehtvee
mechanical pencil	**einen Drehbleistift**	**igh**nern **dray**blighshtift
necklace	**eine Halskette**	**igh**ner **hahls**kehter
pendant	**einen Anhänger**	**igh**nern **ahn**hehngerr
pin	**eine Anstecknadel**	**igh**ner **ahn**shtehknarderl
powder compact	**eine Puderdose**	**igh**ner **poo**derrdoazer
propelling pencil	**einen Drehbleistift**	**igh**nern **dray**blighshtift
ring	**einen Ring**	**igh**nern ring
engagement ring	**Verlobungsring**	fehr**loa**bungsring
signet ring	**Siegelring**	**zee**gerlring
wedding ring	**Ehering**	**ay**erring
rosary	**einen Rosenkranz**	**igh**nern **roa**zernkrahnts
silver plate (silverware)	**Tafelsilber**	**tar**ferlzilberr
snuff box	**eine Schnupftabak-dose**	**igh**ner **shnupf**tahbahk-doazer
strap	**ein Armband**	ighn **ahrm**bahnt
chain strap	**Gliederarmband**	**glee**derrahrmbahnt
leather strap	**Lederarmband**	**lay**derrahrmbahnt
tie clip	**einen Krawatten-klipp**	**igh**nern krah**vah**ternklip
tie pin	**eine Krawatten-nadel**	**igh**ner krah**vah**ternnarderl
vanity case	**ein Ziertäschchen**	ighn **tseer**tehshkhern
watch	**eine Uhr**	**igh**ner oor
pocket watch	**Taschenuhr**	**tah**shernoor
with a second hand	**mit Sekundenzeiger**	mit zeh**kun**derntsighgerr
wristwatch	**Armbanduhr**	**ahrm**bahntoor

SHOPPING GUIDE

Laundry—Dry cleaning

If your hotel doesn't have its own laundry or dry cleaning service, ask the porter:

Where's the nearest laundry/dry cleaner's?	**Wo ist die nächste Wäscherei/chemische Reinigung?**	voa ist dee **nehkh**ster vehsher**righ**/**khay**misher **righ**nigung
I want these clothes...	**Ich möchte diese Kleider ... lassen.**	ikh **murkh**ter **dee**zer **kligh**derr ... **lah**ssern
cleaned	**reinigen**	**righ**niggern
ironed	**bügeln**	**bew**gerln
pressed	**dampfbügeln**	**dahmpf**bewgerln
washed	**waschen**	**vah**shern
When will it be ready?	**Wann ist es fertig?**	vahn ist ehss **fehr**tikh
I need it...	**Ich brauche es...**	ikh **brow**kher ehss
today	**heute**	**hoy**ter
tonight	**heute abend**	**hoy**ter **ar**behrnt
tomorrow	**morgen**	**mor**gern
before Friday	**vor Freitag**	foar **frigh**targ
I want it as soon as possible.	**Ich möchte es so schnell wie möglich.**	ikh **murkh**ter ehss zoa shnehl vee **murg**likh
Can you...this?	**Können Sie das...?**	**kur**nern zee dahss
mend	**ausbessern**	**ows**behssern
patch	**flicken**	**flik**kern
stitch	**nähen**	**nai**ern
Can you sew on this button?	**Können Sie diesen Knopf annähen?**	**kur**nern zee **dee**zern knopf **ahn**naiern
Can you get this stain out?	**Können Sie diesen Fleck entfernen?**	**kur**nern zee **dee**zern flehk ehnt**fehr**nern
Can this be invisibly mended?	**Können Sie das kunststopfen?**	**kur**nern zee dahss **kunst**shtopfern
Is my laundry ready?	**Ist meine Wäsche fertig?**	ist **migh**ner **veh**sher **fehr**tikh
This isn't mine.	**Das gehört nicht mir.**	dahss ger**hurrt** nikht meer
There's one piece missing.	**Es fehlt ein Stück.**	ehss faylt ighn shtewk
There's a hole in this.	**Da ist ein Loch drin.**	dar ist ighn lokh drin

Photography

I want an inexpensive camera.	**Ich möchte eine preiswerte Kamera.**	ikh **murkhter ighner prighsvayrter kahmehrar**
Show me that one in the window.	**Zeigen Sie mir die aus dem Schaufenster.**	**tsighgern zee meer dee owss daym showfehnsterr**

Film

Film sizes aren't always indicated the same way on the Continent as in the U.S.A. and Great Britain. Listed below you'll find some equivalents and translations which will be useful.

I'd like a...	**Ich hätte gern...**	ikh **heh**ter gehrn
film for this camera	**einen Film für diese Kamera**	**igh**nern film fewr **dee**zer **kah**mehrar
120	**sechs mal sechs (6×6)**	zehks marl zehks
127	**vier mal vier (4×4)**	feer marl feer
135	**vierundzwanzig mal sechsunddreißig (24×36)**	**feer**unttsvahntsikh marl **zehks**untdrighssikh
8-mm film	**einen acht Millimeter Film**	**igh**nern ahkht **mil**limayterr film
regular	**Einfach acht**	**ighn**fahkh ahkht
double 8	**Doppel acht**	**dop**perl ahkht
super 8	**Super acht**	**zoo**perr ahkht
16-mm film	**einen sechzehn Millimeter Film**	**igh**nern **zehkh**tsayn **mil**limayterr film
20 exposures	**zwanzig Aufnahmen**	**tsvahn**tsikh **owf**narmern
36 exposures	**sechsunddreißig Aufnahmen**	**zehks**untdrighssikh **owf**narmern
this ASA/DIN number	**diese ASA/DIN Zahl**	**dee**zer **ar**zar/deen tsarl
fast	**höchstempfindlich**	**hurkhst**ehmpfindlikh
fine grain	**Feinkorn**	**fighn**korn
black and white	**schwarzweiß**	shvahrts**vighss**
colour	**Farbfilm**	**fahrp**film
colour negative	**Farbnegativ**	**fahrp**nehgahteef
colour slide	**Farbdiapositive**	**fahrp**deeahpoazitteever
artificial light type	**Kunstlichtfilm**	**kunst**likhtfilm
daylight type	**Tageslichtfilm**	**tar**gerslikhtfilm
Does the price include developing?	**Ist das Entwickeln im Preis inbegriffen?**	ist dahss ehnt**vik**kerln im prighss **in**bergriffern

FOR NUMBERS, see page 175

Processing

How much do you charge for developing?	**Was kostet das Entwickeln?**	vahss **kos**tert dahss ehnt**vik**kerln
I want... prints of each negative.	**Ich möchte... Abzüge von jedem Negativ.**	ikh **murkh**ter ... **ahp**zewger fon **yay**derm **neh**gahteef
with a mat finish	**matt**	maht
with a glossy finish	**Hochglanz**	**hokh**glahnts
Will you please enlarge this?	**Können Sie das bitte vergrößern?**	**kur**nern zee dahss **bit**ter fehr**grur**sserrn
When will it be ready?	**Wann ist es fertig?**	vahn ist ehss **fehr**tikh

Accessories and repairs

I want a/some...	**Ich möchte...**	ikh **murkh**ter
flash bulbs	**Blitzlampen**	**blits**lahmpern
flash cubes	**Blitzwürfel**	**blits**vewrferl
for black and white	**für schwarzweiß**	fewr shvahrts**vighss**
for colour	**für Farbe**	fewr **fahr**ber
lens cap	**einen Objektivdeckel**	**igh**nern obyehk**teef**dehkerl
lens cleaners	**Objektivreiniger**	obyehk**teef**righnigerr
red filter	**einen Rotfilter**	**igh**nern **roat**filterr
yellow filter	**einen Gelbfilter**	**igh**nern **gehlp**filterr
ultra-violet filter	**einen Ultraviolett-filter**	**igh**nern **ul**trahvioaleht-filterr
Can you repair this camera?	**Können Sie diese Kamera reparieren?**	**kur**nern zee **dee**zer **kah**mehrar rehpah**reer**ern
The film is jammed.	**Der Film klemmt.**	dehr film klehmt
There's something wrong with the...	**Mit... stimmt etwas nicht.**	mit ... shtimt **eht**vahss nikht
exposure counter	**dem Bildzählwerk**	daym **bilt**tsailvehrk
film winder	**dem Transportknopf**	daym trahns**port**knopf
flash contact	**dem Blitzkontakt**	daym **blits**kontahkt
lens	**dem Objektiv**	daym obyehk**teef**
light meter	**dem Belichtungs-messer**	daym ber**likh**tungsmehsserr
rangefinder	**dem Entfernungs-messer**	daym ehnt**fehr**nungsmehsser
shutter	**dem Verschluß**	daym fehr**shluss**

Provisions

Here's a basic list of food and drink that you might want on a picnic or for the occasional meal at home:

I'd like some..., please.	**Ich möchte bitte...**	ikh **murkh**ter **bit**ter
apple juice	**Apfelsaft**	**ah**pferlzahft
apples	**Äpfel**	**eh**pferl
bananas	**Bananen**	bah**nar**nern
biscuits (Br.)	**Kekse**	**kayk**ser
bread	**Brot**	broat
butter	**Butter**	**butt**err
cake	**Kuchen**	**koo**khern
candy	**Konfekt**	kon**fehkt**
cheese	**Käse**	**kai**zer
chocolate	**Schokolade**	shokkol**lar**der
coffee	**Kaffee**	**kah**fay
cold cuts	**Aufschnitt**	**owf**shnit
cookies	**Kekse**	**kayk**ser
cooking fat	**Kochfett**	**kokh**feht
crackers	**Cräckers**	**kreh**kerr
crisps	**Kartoffelchips**	kahr**toff**erlchips
cucumbers	**Gurken**	**goor**kern
eggs	**Eier**	**igh**err
flour	**Mehl**	mayl
frankfurters	**Frankfurter Würstchen**	**frahnk**foorterr **vewrst**khern
grapefruit juice	**Pampelmusensaft**	pahmperl**moo**zernzahft
grapefruits	**Pampelmusen**	pahmperl**moo**zern
ham	**Schinken**	**shing**kern
ice-cream	**Eis**	ighss
lemons	**Zitronen**	tsi**troa**nern
lettuce	**Kopfsalat**	**kopf**zahlart
liver sausage	**Leberwurst**	**lay**berrvoorst
milk	**Milch**	milkh
mustard	**Senf**	zehnf
oil	**Öl**	url
orange juice	**Apfelsinensaft**	ahpferl**zee**nernzahft
oranges	**Apfelsinen**	ahpferl**zee**nern
pepper	**Pfeffer**	**pfeh**ferr
pickles	**Essiggemüse**	**eh**ssikhgermewzer
potato chips	**Kartoffelchips**	kahr**toff**erlchips
potatoes	**Kartoffeln**	kahr**toff**erln
rolls	**Brötchen**	**brurt**khern
salad	**Salat**	zah**lart**

salami	**Salami**	zah**lar**mee
salt	**Salz**	zahlts
sandwiches	**Sandwichs**	**zehnt**vichs
sausages	**Würstchen**	**vewrst**khern
spaghetti	**Spaghetti**	spah**geh**tee
sugar	**Zucker**	**tsuk**kerr
sweets	**Konfekt**	kon**fehkt**
tea	**Tee**	tay
tomato juice	**Tomatensaft**	tom**mar**ternzahft
tomatoes	**Tomaten**	tom**mar**tern
yoghurt	**Joghurt**	**yoa**goort

And don't forget...

a bottle opener	**einen Flaschenöffner**	**igh**nern **flah**shernurfnerr
a corkscrew	**einen Korkenzieher**	**igh**nern **kor**kerntseeherr
matches	**Streichhölzer**	**shtrighkh**hurltserr
paper napkins	**Papierservietten**	pah**peer**zehrviehtern
a tin (can) opener	**einen Büchsenöffner**	**igh**nern **bewk**sernurfnerr

Weights and measures

1 kilogram or kilo (kg) = 1000 grams (g)

100 g = 3.5 oz. ½ kg = 1.1 lb.
200 g = 7.0 oz. 1 kg = 2.2 lb.

1 oz. = 28.35 g
1 lb. = 453.60 g

1 litre (l) = 0.88 imp. quarts = 1.06 U.S. quarts

1 imp. quart = 1.14 l 1 U.S. quart = 0.95 l
1 imp. gallon = 4.55 l 1 U.S. gallon = 3.8 l

bottle	**die Flasche**	dee **flah**sher
box	**die Schachtel**	dee **shahkh**terl
can	**die Büchse/Dose**	dee **bewk**ser/**doa**zer
carton	**die Packung**	dee **pah**kung
crate	**die Kiste**	dee **kis**ter
jar	**das Glas**	dahss glahss
packet	**die Packung**	dee **pah**kung
tin	**die Büchse/Dose**	dee **bewk**ser/**doa**zer
tube	**die Tube**	dee **too**ber

Souvenirs

Here are some suggestions for articles which you may wish to buy as gifts or souvenirs when in Germany:

Bavarian peasant dress	**das Dirndl (Kleid)**	dahss **deerndl**(klight)
beer stein	**der Bierkrug**	derr **beer**kroog
camera	**die Kamera**	dee **kah**mehrar
cutlery	**das Tafelbesteck**	dahss **tar**ferlbershtehk
doll	**die Puppe**	dee **pup**per
glassware	**die Glaswaren**	dee **glahs**varrern
leather goods	**die Lederwaren**	dee **lay**derrvarrern
music box	**die Spieldose**	dee **shpeel**doazer
porcelain	**das Porzellan**	dahss portseh**larn**
silver plate (silverware)	**das Tafelsilber**	dahss **tar**ferlzilberr
toy	**das Spielzeug**	dahss **shpeel**tsoyg
waterproof woollen overcoat	**der Lodenmantel**	derr **loa**dernmahnterl
wood carving	**die Holzschnitzarbeit**	dee **holts**shnitsahrbight

Remember to find out whether you're entitled to reimbursement of value-added tax *(Mehrwertsteuer)* for the article you bought. A 10-percent rebate may be obtained for certain items by declaring them at the customs when leaving Germany. (So far there's no VAT in Austria and Switzerland.) You should ask for details about this at the time of purchase.

The high quality of Austrian and Swiss winter sports equipment is well known. But petit-point embroidery and porcelain in Austria and linens and organdies in Switzerland easily catch the feminine eye. Look into leather goods and *Lederhosen* (knee-length leather trousers) in Austria while not missing the fabulous array of watches and luscious chocolate in Switzerland.

chocolate	**die Schokolade**	dee shokkol**lar**der
cuckoo clock	**die Kuckucksuhr**	dee **kuk**kuksoor
embroidery	**die Stickerei**	dee shtikker**righ**
linen	**das Leinenzeug**	dahss **ligh**nerntsoyg
ski equipment	**die Schiausrüstung**	dee **shee**owsrewstung
Tyrolean hat	**der Tirolerhut**	derr tee**roa**lerrhoot
Tyrolean pipe	**die Tiroler Pfeife**	dee tee**roa**lerr **pfigh**fer
watch	**die Uhr**	dee **oor**

Tobacconist's

As at home, cigarettes are generally referred to by their brand names, e.g., *Ernte* (**ehrn**ter), *HB* (har **bay**) and *Rothändle* (**roat**hehndler).

Give me a / an / some..., please.	**Geben Sie mir bitte...**	**gay**bern zee meer **bit**ter
ashtray	**einen Aschenbecher**	**igh**nern **ah**shernbehkherr
chewing tobacco	**Kautabak**	**kow**tahbahk
cigar	**eine Zigarre**	**igh**ner tsig**gah**rer
cigars	**ein paar Zigarren**	ighn parr tsig**gah**rern
cigarette case	**ein Zigarettenetui**	ighn tsiggah**reh**ternehtvee
cigarette holder	**eine Zigaretten-spitze**	**igh**ner tsiggah**reh**tern-shpitser
cigarette lighter	**ein Feuerzeug**	ighn **foy**errtsoyg
flints	**Feuersteine**	**foy**errshtighner
humidor	**einen Tabaktopf**	**igh**nern tah**bahk**topf
lighter fluid	**Feuerzeugbenzin**	**foy**errtsoygbehntseen
lighter gas	**Feuerzeuggas**	**foy**errtsoyggarss
matches	**Streichhölzer**	**shtrighkh**hurltserr
packet of cigarettes	**eine Schachtel Zigaretten**	**igh**ner **shahkh**terl tsiggah**reh**tern
packet of...	**eine Schachtel...**	**igh**ner **shahkh**terl
pipe	**eine Pfeife**	**igh**ner **pfigh**fer
pipe cleaners	**Pfeifenreiniger**	**pfigh**fernrighniggerr
pipe rack	**einen Pfeifen-ständer**	**igh**nern **pfigh**fern-shtehnderr
pipe tobacco	**Pfeifentabak**	**pfigh**ferntahbahk
pipe tool	**ein Pfeifenbesteck**	ighn **pfigh**fernbehshtehk
snuff	**Schnupftabak**	**shnupf**tahbahk
tobacco pouch	**einen Tabakbeutel**	**igh**nern tah**bahk**boyterl
wick	**einen Docht**	**igh**nern dokht
Do you have any...?	**Haben Sie...?**	**har**bern zee
American cigarettes	**amerikanische Zigaretten**	ahmehri**kar**nisher tsiggah**reh**tern
English cigarettes	**englische Zigaretten**	**ehng**lisher tsiggah**reh**tern
menthol cigarettes	**Mentholzigaretten**	mehn**toal**tsiggahrehtern

filter tipped	**mit Filter**	mit **fil**terr
without filter	**ohne Filter**	**oa**ner **fil**terr
king-size	**extra lang**	**ehk**strar lahng

I'll take two packets.	**Ich nehme zwei Schachteln.**	ikh **nay**mer tsvigh **shahkh**terln
I'd like a carton.	**Ich möchte eine Stange.**	ikh **murkh**ter **igh**ner **shtahng**er

While we're on the subject of cigarettes, suppose you want to offer somebody one?

Would you like a cigarette?	**Darf ich Ihnen eine Zigarette anbieten?**	dahrf ikh **ee**nern **igh**ner tsiggah**reh**ter **ahn**beetern
Have one of mine.	**Nehmen Sie eine von meinen.**	**nay**mern zee **igh**ner fon **migh**nern
Try one of these.	**Versuchen Sie mal eine von diesen.**	fehr**zoo**khern zee marl **igh**ner fon **dee**zern
They're very mild.	**Sie sind sehr mild.**	zee zint zayr milt
They're a bit strong.	**Sie sind ziemlich stark.**	zee zint **tseem**likh shtahrk

And if somebody offers you one?

Thank you.	**Danke.**	**dahng**ker
No, thanks.	**Nein danke.**	nighn **dahng**ker
I don't smoke.	**Ich rauche nicht.**	ikh **row**kher nikht
I've given it up.	**Ich rauche nicht mehr.**	ikh **row**kher nikht mayr

Your money: banks—currency

In banks in the larger towns there's sure to be someone who speaks English. Banks are generally open Monday to Friday from 8 a.m. till noon and from 2 to 4 p.m.

The *Deutsche Mark* (abbreviated to *DM* and called *D-Mark*—**day** mahrk) is the unit of currency in Germany. It's divided into 100 *Pfennig* (**pfeh**nikh). There are coins of 1 and 2 pfennigs (rare nowadays) and 5, 10 and 50 pfennigs and of 1, 2 and 5 marks. Banknotes: 5, 10, 20, 50, 100, 500 and 1000 marks.

In Austria, the basic unit is the *Schilling* (**shil**ling), abbreviated *S*. It's divided into 100 *Groschen* (**gro**shern), abbreviated *g*. Coin denominations are as follows: 1, 2, 5, 10, 20 and 50 groschen and 1, 5 and 10 schillings. There are banknotes of 20, 50, 100, 500 and 1000 schillings.

The *Franken* (**frahng**kern), usually abbreviated *Fr.*, is the Swiss unit of currency. There are 100 *Rappen* (**rah**pern) , abbreviated *Rp.*, to a franc. Coins are of 5, 10, 20 and 50 Rappen and 1, 2 and 5 franc denominations. Banknotes: 10, 20, 50, 100, 500 and 1000 francs.

In Germany, as well as in Austria and Switzerland, you'll find numerous small currency-exchange offices, indicated by the words *Geldwechsel* or *Wechselstube*. Sometimes they're open outside regular banking hours.

Where's the nearest bank?	**Wo ist die nächste Bank?**	voa ist dee **nehkh**ster bahngk
Where can I find a currency-exchange office?	**Wo finde ich eine Wechselstube?**	voa **fin**der ikh **igh**ner **vehk**serlshtoober
Where's the "Commerzbank"?	**Wo ist die «Commerzbank»?**	voa ist dee kom**mehrts**bahngk
Where can I cash a traveller's cheque (check)?	**Wo kann ich einen Reisescheck einlösen?**	voa kahn ikh **igh**nern **righ**zershehk **ighn**lurzern'

Inside

I want to change some dollars.	**Ich möchte einige Dollar wechseln.**	ikh **murkh**ter **igh**nigger **dol**lar **vehk**serln
I'd like to change some pounds.	**Ich möchte einige Pfund wechseln.**	ikh **murkh**ter **igh**nigger pfunt **vehk**serln
Here's my passport.	**Hier ist mein Paß.**	heer ist mighn pahss
What's the exchange rate?	**Wie ist der Wechselkurs?**	vee ist derr **vehk**serlkoorss
What rate of commission do you charge?	**Welche Gebühr erheben Sie?**	**wehl**kher ger**bewr** ehr**hay**bern zee
Can you cash a personal cheque?	**Können Sie einen Barscheck einlösen?**	**kur**nern zee **igh**nern **barr**shehk **ighn**lurzern
How long will it take to clear?	**Wie lange brauchen Sie für die Überprüfung?**	vee **lahn**ger **brow**khern zee fewr dee ewberr**prew**fung
Can you wire my bank in London?	**Können Sie meiner Bank in London telegraphieren?**	**kur**nern zee **migh**nerr bahngk in **lon**don taylaygrah**fee**rern
I have...	**Ich habe...**	ikh **har**ber
a letter of credit	**einen Kreditbrief**	**igh**nern kray**dit**breef
an introduction from...	**einen Empfehlungsbrief von...**	**igh**nern ehm**pfay**lungsbreef fon
a credit card	**eine Kreditkarte**	**igh**ner kray**dit**kahrter
I'm expecting some money from Boston. Has it arrived yet?	**Ich erwarte Geld aus Boston. Ist es schon angekommen?**	ikh ehr**vahr**ter gehlt owss **bos**ton. ist ehss shoan **ahn**gerkommern
Please give me... notes (bills) and some small change.	**Geben Sie mir bitte... Scheine und etwas Kleingeld.**	**gay**bern zee meer **bit**ter ... **shigh**ner unt **eht**vahss **klighn**gehlt
Give me... large notes and the rest in small notes.	**Geben Sie mir... große Scheine und den Rest in kleinen Scheinen.**	**gay**bern zee meer ... **groas**ser **shigh**ner unt dayn rehst in **kligh**nern **shigh**nern
Could you please check that again?	**Könnten Sie das bitte nochmal nachrechnen?**	**kurn**tern zee dahss **bit**ter **nokh**marl **nahkh**rehkhnern

Depositing

I want to credit this to my account.	**Ich möchte das auf mein Konto einzahlen.**	ikh **murkh**ter dahss owf mighn **kon**toa **ighn**tsarlern
I want to credit this to Mr...'s account.	**Ich möchte dies auf das Konto von Herrn... einzahlen.**	ikh **murkh**ter deess owf dahss **kon**toa fon hehrn ... **ighn**tsarlern
Where should I sign?	**Wo muß ich unterschreiben?**	voa muss ikh unterr**shrigh**bern

Currency converter

In a world of floating currencies, we can offer no more than this do-it-yourself chart. You can get a card showing current exchange rates from banks, travel agents and tourist offices. Why not fill in this chart, too, for handy reference?

	£	$
1 German mark 5 20 50 100		
1 Austrian shilling 5 20 50 100		
1 Swiss franc 5 20 50 100		

At the post-office

The offices of Germany's *Bundespost* are open from 8 a.m. to midday and from 2 to 6.30 p.m. They close at noon on Saturdays. Mail-boxes in Germany are painted yellow. Swiss post-offices are open from 7.30 a.m. to midday and from 1.30 to 6.30 p.m. (8 to 11 a.m. on Saturdays). Mail-boxes are yellow. In Austria, post-offices are open from 8 a.m. to midday and from 2 to 5 p.m. (8 to 10 a.m. on Saturdays). Austrian mail-boxes are yellow or blue.

In principal cities, some post-offices are open outside the normal hours. Remember that for telephoning and cables you should go to the post-office—there are no separate telephone or cable offices.

Where's the nearest post-office?	**Wo ist das nächste Postamt?**	voa ist dahss **nehkh**ster **post**ahmt
What time does the post-office open/close?	**Wann wird das Postamt geöffnet/geschlossen?**	vahn veert dahss **post**ahmt ger**urf**nert/ger**shlo**ssern
What window do I go to for stamps?	**An welchem Schalter gibt es Briefmarken?**	ahn **vehl**kherm **shahl**terr gipt ehss **breef**mahrkern
At which counter can I cash an international money order?	**An welchem Schalter kann ich eine internationale Postanweisung einlösen?**	ahn **vehl**kherm **shahl**terr kahn ikh **igh**ner interrnahtsioa**nar**ler **post**ahnvighzung **ighn**lurzern
I want... 40-pfennig stamps.	**Ich möchte... Briefmarken zu 40 Pfennig.**	ikh **murkh**ter... **breef**mahrkern tsu 40 **pfeh**nikh
What's the postage for a letter/a postcard to London?	**Was kostet ein Brief/eine Postkarte nach London?**	vahss **kos**tert ighn breef/**igh**ner **post**kahrter nahkh **lon**don
Do I need to fill in a customs declaration?	**Muß ich ein Zollerklärungs-formular ausfüllen?**	muss ikh ighn **tsoll**-ehrklairungsformullarr **ows**fewlern

Do all letters go airmail?	**Gehen alle Briefe per Luftpost?**	gayern **ah**ler **bree**fer pehr **luft**post
I want to send this parcel.	**Ich möchte ein Paket aufgeben.**	ikh **murkh**ter ighn pah**kayt owf**gaybern
Where's the mail-box?	**Wo ist der Briefkasten?**	voa ist derr **breef**kahstern
I want to send this by...	**Ich möchte dies... senden.**	ikh **murkh**ter deess... **zehn**dern
airmail	**per Luftpost**	pehr **luft**post
express (special delivery)	**per Eilboten**	pehr **ighl**boatern
registered mail	**eingeschrieben**	**ighn**gershreebern
Where's the poste restante (general delivery)?	**Wo ist der Schalter für postlagernde Sendungen?**	voa ist derr **shahl**terr fewr **post**largerrnder **zehn**dungern
Is there any mail for me? My name is...	**Ist Post für mich da? Ich heiße...**	ist post fewr mikh dar? ikh **high**sser

BRIEFMARKEN	STAMPS
PAKETE	PARCELS
POSTANWEISUNGEN	MONEY ORDERS

Cables (telegrams)

I want to send a telegram. May I please have a form?	**Ich möchte ein Telegramm aufgeben. Kann ich bitte ein Formular haben?**	ikh **murkh**ter ighn taylay**grahm owf**gaybern. kahn ikh **bi**tter ighn formul**larr har**bern
How much is it per word?	**Was kostet es pro Wort?**	vahss **kos**tert ehss proa vort
How long will a cable to Chicago take?	**Wie lange braucht ein Telegramm nach Chicago?**	vee **lahng**er browkht ighn taylay**grahm** nahkh tshik**kar**goa
I'd like to send a night-letter.	**Ich möchte ein Brieftelegramm aufgeben.**	ikh **murkh**ter ighn **breef**-taylaygrahm **owf**gaybern

POST-OFFICE

Telephoning

In Germany and Switzerland, the telephone network is virtually fully automatic, and instructions are posted in every telephone booth.

In Austria there are still some out-of-the-way places where you may have to phone via an operator. In this case, you merely lift the receiver and wait for the operator to answer.

Phone numbers are given in pairs. Long distance calls may be placed by the hotel or by going directly to the post-office. From most cities you can also make automatic calls within Europe and overseas.

Note: In telephoning, *zwei* becomes *zwo* (tsvoa).

Where's the telephone?	**Wo ist das Telephon?**	voa ist dahss taylay**foan**
Where's the nearest telephone booth?	**Wo ist die nächste Telephonzelle?**	voa ist dee **nehkh**ster taylay**foan**tsehler
May I use your phone?	**Darf ich Ihr Telephon benutzen?**	dahrf ikh eer taylay**foan** bernutsern
Do you have a telephone directory for Bonn?	**Haben Sie ein Telephonbuch von Bonn?**	**har**bern zee ighn taylay**foan**bukh fon bon
Can you help me get this number?	**Können Sie mir helfen, diese Nummer zu bekommen?**	**kur**nern zee meer **hehl**fern **dee**zer **num**merr tsu ber**kom**mern

Operator

Do you speak English?	**Sprechen Sie Englisch?**	**shpreh**khern zee **ehng**lish
Good morning, I want Hamburg 123456.	**Guten Morgen. Ich möchte Hamburg 123456.**	**goo**tern **mor**gern. ikh **murkh**ter **hahm**boorg 123456
Can I dial direct?	**Kann ich durchwählen?**	kahn ikh **doorkh**vailern
I want to place a personal (person-to-person) call.	**Ich möchte ein Gespräch mit Voranmeldung.**	ikh **murkh**ter ighn ger**shpraikh** mit **foar**ahnmehldung

FOR NUMBERS, see page 175

I want to reverse the charges.	**Ich möchte ein R-Gespräch anmelden.**	ikh **murkh**ter ighn **ehr**-gershpraikh **ahn**mehldern
Will you tell me the cost of the call afterwards?	**Würden Sie mir anschließend die Gebühr mitteilen?**	**vewr**dern zee meer **ahn**shleessernt dee ger**bewr mit**tighlern

Telephone alphabet

A	**Anton**	**ahn**toan	O	**Otto**	**ot**toa
Ä	**Ärger**	**ehr**gerr	Ö	**Ökonom**	urkoa**noam**
B	**Berta**	**behr**tar	P	**Paula**	**pow**lah
C	**Caesar**	**tsai**zahr	Q	**Quelle**	**kveh**ler
CH	**Charlotte**	shahr**lot**ter	R	**Richard**	**rik**hahrt
D	**Dora**	**doa**rah	S	**Samuel**	**zar**muehl
E	**Emil**	ay**meel**	SCH	**Schule**	**shoo**ler
F	**Friedrich**	**free**drikh	T	**Theodor**	**tay**oadoar
G	**Gustav**	**gus**tahf	U	**Ulrich**	**ul**rikh
H	**Heinrich**	**highn**rikh	Ü	**Übel**	**ew**berl
I	**Ida**	**ee**dah	V	**Viktor**	**vik**toar
J	**Julius**	**yoo**liuss	W	**Wilhelm**	**vil**hehlm
K	**Kaufmann**	**kowf**mahn	X	**Xanthippe**	ksahn**tip**per
L	**Ludwig**	**lud**vig	Y	**Ypsilon**	**ewp**zeeloan
M	**Martha**	**mahr**tah	Z	**Zacharias**	tsahkhah**ree**ahss
N	**Nordpol**	**nort**poal			

Speaking

Hello. This is... speaking.	**Hallo. Hier spricht...**	**hah**loa. heer shprikht
I want to speak to...	**Ich möchte... sprechen.**	ikh **murkh**ter **shpreh**khern
Would you put me through to...?	**Verbinden Sie mich bitte mit...**	fehr**bin**dern zee mikh **bit**ter mit
I want extension...	**Ich möchte Nebenanschluß...**	ikh **murkh**ter **nay**bern-ahnshluss
Is that...?	**Ist dort...?**	ist dort

Bad luck

Would you please try again later?	**Würden Sie es bitte später noch einmal versuchen?**	**vewr**dern zee ehss **bit**ter **shpai**terr nokh **ighn**marl fehr**zoo**khern

TELEPHONE

Operator, you gave me the wrong number.	**Fräulein, Sie haben mich falsch verbunden.**	froylighn zee harbern mikh fahlsh fehrbundern
We were cut off.	**Wir sind unterbrochen worden.**	veer zint unterrbrokhern vordern

Not there

When will he/she be back?	**Wann kommt er/sie zurück?**	vahn komt ehr/zee tsoorewk
Will you tell him/her I called? My name's...	**Würden Sie ihm/ihr sagen, daß ich angerufen habe? Mein Name ist...**	vewrdern zee eem/eer zargern dahss ikh ahngerroofern harber? mighn narmer ist
Would you ask him/her to call me?	**Würden Sie ihn/sie bitten, mich anzurufen?**	vewrdern zee een/zee bittern mikh ahntsooroofern
Would you please take a message?	**Würden Sie bitte etwas ausrichten?**	vewrdern zee bitter ehtvahss owsrikhtern

Charges

What was the cost of that call?	**Was hat das Gespräch gekostet?**	vahss haht dahss gershpraikh gerkostert
I want to pay for the call.	**Ich möchte das Gespräch bezahlen.**	ikh murkhter dahss gershpraikh bertsarlern

Ein Anruf für Sie.	There's a telephone call for you.
Welche Nummer haben Sie gewählt?	What number are you calling?
Die Linie ist besetzt.	The line's engaged.
Es meldet sich niemand.	There's no answer.
Sie sind falsch verbunden.	You've got the wrong number.
Das Telephon funktioniert nicht.	The phone is out of order.
Er/Sie ist im Augenblick nicht da.	He's/She's out at the moment.

The car

Filling station

We'll start this section by considering your possible needs at a filling station. Most of them don't handle major repairs; but apart from providing you with fuel, they may be helpful in solving all kinds of minor problems.

Where's the nearest filling station?	**Wo ist die nächste Tankstelle?**	voa ist dee **nehkh**ster **tahnk**shtehler
I want 20 litres of petrol (gas), please.	**Ich möchte 20 Liter Benzin, bitte.**	ikh **murkh**ter 20 **lee**terr behn**tseen bit**ter
I want 30 litres of standard/premium.	**Ich möchte 30 Liter Normal/Super.**	ikh **murkh**ter 30 **lee**terr nor**marl**/**zoo**perr
Give me 25 marks worth of...	**Für 25 Mark...**	fewr 25 mahrk
Fill her up, please.	**Voll, bitte.**	fol **bit**ter
Please check the oil and water.	**Kontrollieren Sie bitte Ölstand und Wasser.**	kontrol**lee**rern zee **bit**ter **url**shtahnt unt **vah**sserr
Give me 2 litres of oil.	**Geben Sie mir 2 Liter Öl.**	**gay**bern zee meer 2 **lee**terr url
Fill up the battery with distilled water.	**Füllen Sie bitte destilliertes Wasser in der Batterie nach.**	**few**lern zee **bit**ter dehstil**leer**terss **vah**sser in derr bahteh**ree** nahkh
Check the brake fluid.	**Kontrollieren Sie die Bremsflüssigkeit.**	kontrol**lee**rern zee dee **brehms**flewssikhkight

Fluid measures					
litres	imp. gal.	U.S. gal.	litres	imp. gal.	U.S. gal.
5	1.1	1.3	30	6.6	7.8
10	2.2	2.6	35	7.7	9.1
15	3.3	3.9	40	8.8	10.4
20	4.4	5.2	45	9.9	11.7
25	5.5	6.5	50	11.0	13.0

FOR NUMBERS, see page 175

Would you check the tire pressure?	**Würden Sie bitte den Reifendruck prüfen?**	**vewr**dern zee **bit**ter dayn **righ**ferndruk **prew**fern
1.6 front, 1.8 rear.	**Vorne 1,6, hinten 1,8.***	**for**ner 1,6 **hin**tern 1,8

Tire pressure			
lb./sq. in.	kg./cm.²	lb./sq. in.	kg./cm.²
10	0.7	26	1.8
12	0.8	27	1.9
15	1.1	28	2.0
18	1.3	30	2.1
20	1.4	33	2.3
21	1.5	36	2.5
23	1.6	38	2.7
24	1.7	40	2.8

Please check the spare tire, too.	**Prüfen Sie auch den Ersatzreifen, bitte.**	**prew**fern zee owkh dayn **ehr**zahtsrighfern **bit**ter
Can you mend this puncture (fix this flat)?	**Können Sie diesen Reifen flicken?**	**kur**nern zee **dee**zern **righ**fern **flik**kern
Would you please change this tire?	**Würden Sie bitte diesen Reifen wechseln?**	**vewr**dern zee **bit**ter **dee**zern **righ**fern **vehk**serln
Would you clean the windscreen (windshield)?	**Würden Sie bitte die Windschutzscheibe reinigen?**	**vewr**dern zee **bit**ter dee **vint**shutsshighber **righ**niggern
Have you a road map of this district?	**Haben Sie eine Straßenkarte von dieser Gegend?**	**har**bern zee **igh**ner **shtrar**ssernkahrter fon **dee**zerr **gay**gernt
Where are the toilets?	**Wo sind die Toiletten?**	voa zint dee toaah**leh**tern

* Germans don't say, for instance, one *point* eight but simply one eight (*eins acht* – ighns ahkht) or one *comma* eight (*eins komma acht* – ighns kommah ahkht).

Asking the way—Street directions

Excuse me.	**Entschuldigung.**	ehnts**hul**diggung
Can you tell me the way to...?	**Können Sie mir sagen, wie ich nach... komme?**	**kur**nern zee meer **zar**gern vee ikh nahkh ...**kom**mer
How do I get to...?	**Wie komme ich nach...?**	vee **kom**mer ikh nahkh
Where does this road lead to?	**Wohin führt diese Straße?**	voa**hin** fewrt **dee**zer **shtrah**sser
Are we on the right road for...?	**Sind wir auf der richtigen Straße nach...?**	zint veer owf derr **rikh**tiggern **shtrah**sser nahkh
How far is the next village?	**Wie weit ist es bis zum nächsten Dorf?**	vee vight ist ehss biss tsum **nehkh**stern dorf
How far is it to... from here?	**Wie weit ist es von hier nach...?**	vee vight ist ehss fon heer nahkh
Can you tell me, where... is?	**Können Sie mir sagen, wo... ist?**	**kur**nern zee meer **zar**gern voa ... ist
Where can I find this address?	**Wie komme ich zu dieser Adresse?**	vee **kom**mer ikh tsu **dee**zer ahd**reh**sser
Where's this?	**Wo ist das?**	voa ist dahss

Miles into kilometres

1 mile = 1.609 kilometres (km.)

miles	10	20	30	40	50	60	70	80	90	100
km.	16	32	48	64	80	97	113	129	145	161

Kilometres into miles

1 kilometre (km.) = 0.62 miles

km.	10	20	30	40	50	60	70	80	90	100	110	120	130
miles	6	12	19	25	31	37	44	50	56	62	68	75	81

CAR – INFORMATION

Can you show me on the map where I am?	**Können Sie mir auf der Karte zeigen, wo ich bin?**	**kur**nern zee meer owf derr **kahr**ter **tsigh**gern voa ikh bin
Can you show me on the map where the university is?	**Können Sie mir auf der Karte zeigen, wo die Universität ist?**	**kur**nern zee meer owf derr **kahr**ter **tsigh**gern voa dee unnivvehrzit**tait** ist
Can I park there?	**Kann man dort parken?**	kahn mahn dort **pahr**kern
Is that a one-way street?	**Ist das eine Einbahnstraße?**	ist dahss **igh**ner **ighn**barnshtrarsser
Does the traffic go this way?	**Ist dies die Fahrtrichtung?**	ist deess dee **farrt**-rikhtung

Sie sind auf der falschen Straße.	You're on the wrong road.
Fahren Sie geradeaus.	Go straight ahead.
Es ist dort unten...	It's down there on the...
links/rechts	left/right
Fahren Sie bis zur ersten (zweiten) Kreuzung.	Go to the first (second) crossroads.
Biegen Sie bei der Ampel links ab.	Turn left at the traffic lights.
Biegen Sie bei der nächsten Ecke rechts ab.	Turn right at the next corner.

In the rest of this section we'll be more closely concerned with the car itself. We've divided it into two parts:

Part A contains general advice on motoring in Germany, Austria and Switzerland. It's essentially for reference and is therefore to be browsed over, preferably in advance.

Part B is concerned with the practical details of accidents and breakdown. It includes a list of car parts and a list of things that may go wrong with them. All you have to do is to show it to the garage mechanic and get him to point to the items required.

Part A

Customs—Documentation

You'll need the following documents when driving in Germany, Austria and Switzerland:

passport
international insurance certificate (green card)
log book (car registration card)
valid driving licence

The nationality plate or sticker must be on the car. Since some countries require a translation of your home driving licence, an international driving permit may save you trouble.

A red warning triangle—for display on the road in case of accident—is compulsory; parking lights are advisable. Crash helmets are mandatory for both riders and passengers on motorcycles and scooters.

Here's my...	**Hier ist...**	heer ist
customs pass	**meine Zollbescheinigung**	**migh**ner **tsol**bershigh-niggung
driving licence	**mein Führerschein**	mighn **few**rerrshighn
green card	**meine grüne Versicherungskarte**	**migh**ner **grew**ner fehr-zikherrungskahrter
passport	**mein Paß**	mighn pahss
log book (car registration card)	**mein Kraftfahrzeugschein**	mighn **krahft**fahrtsoyg-shighn

Driving

The classification of roads in Germany is as follows:

E. 4	**Europastraße**—international road or motorway (turnpike)
BAB	**Bundesautobahn** motorway (turnpike)
B. 5	**Bundesstraße**—first-class main road
L. 162	**Landesstraße**—second-class main road
K. 27	**Kreisstraße**—district road

The roads are good in Germany, Austria and Switzerland. There's an extensive network of motorways (turnpikes), which are all toll-free. At regular intervals along many motorways there are 24-hour telephone posts for emergencies, breakdown and accidents.

The same rules and regulations as in Germany generally apply on Austrian and Swiss roads. But on mountain roads there are some courtesies to be kept in mind: when two vehicles meet on very narrow roads the ascending vehicle has priority over the descending one. Try to keep a lookout ahead so that you can pull in to the side at some suitable spot before meeting the other vehicle. You must wherever possible give way to busses and other heavy vehicles.

As half of Switzerland and three-fourths of Austria are mountainous, don't forget to exercice particular caution on mountain roads where visibility may be impaired due to sharp bends and haze. In winter, make sure to check on driving conditions as some roads are temporarily closed, and wintry storms can make roads hazardous from October to May. Snow tires or chains are obligatory in some areas. In winter, if you dial 163 in Switzerland, a recorded message in German reports current road conditions for the region. As in Germany, you'll find roads in Austria and Switzerland usually very well paved and marked for the motorist—though village roads may be narrow and require careful driving.

The police are normally quite lenient with tourists, but don't push your luck too far. For small offences you can be fined on the spot. Here are some phrases which may come in handy in case of confrontation with the *Polizei.* If you're in serious trouble, insist on an interpreter.

I'm sorry, officer, I didn't see the sign.	**Es tut mir leid, ich habe das Zeichen nicht gesehen.**	ehss toot meer light ikh **har**ber dahss **tsigh**khern nikht ger**zay**ern
The light was green.	**Die Ampel war grün.**	dee **ahm**perl varr grewn
I'm sorry, I don't speak German very well.	**Es tut mir leid, ich spreche nur wenig Deutsch.**	ehss toot meer light ikh **shpreh**kher noor **vay**nikh doych
I don't understand.	**Ich verstehe nicht.**	ikh vehr**shtay**er nikht
How much is the fine?	**Wie hoch ist die Buße?**	vee hoakh ist dee **boo**sser

Parking

Use your common sense when parking. Park your vehicle in the direction of moving traffic, not against it. Obey the parking regulations which will be indicated by signs or by lines painted on the kerb (curb).

When you park in the mountains in winter it's best to leave your car in gear but not to put the hand brake on. This will prevent the brake shoes from being frozen in in this position.

Excuse me. May I park here?	**Verzeihung, darf ich hier parken?**	fehr**tsigh**ung dahrf ikh heer **pahr**kern
How long can I park here?	**Wie lange kann ich hier parken?**	vee **lahng**er kahn ikh heer **pahr**kern
Do I have to leave my lights on?	**Muß ich das Parklicht brennen lassen?**	muss ikh dahss **pahr**klikht **breh**nern **lah**ssern
Excuse me. Do you have some change for the parking meter?	**Verzeihung, haben Sie zufällig Kleingeld für die Parkuhr?**	fehr**tsigh**ung **har**bern zee **tsoo**fehlikh **kligh**ngehlt fewr dee **pahr**koor

CAR – INFORMATION

Road signs

Listed below are some written signs which you'll certainly encounter when driving in Germany. Obviously, they should be studied in advance. You can't drive and read at the same time!

AUF 10 KM	Indicates that a sign applies for 10 kilometres
BLAUE ZONE	Blue zone (parking); special parking disc required
DURCHGANGSVERKEHR	Through traffic
EINBAHNSTRASSE	One-way street
EINORDNEN	Get in lane
ENDE DES PARKVERBOTS	End of no-parking zone
...ERLAUBT	...permitted
FROSTSCHÄDEN	Ice damage
FUSSGÄNGER	Pedestrians
GEFÄHRLICHES GEFÄLLE	Steep descent
GEFÄHRLICHE STEIGUNG	Steep climb
HALT, POLIZEI	Stop, police
HUPEN VERBOTEN	No honking
KEIN DURCHGANG FÜR FUSSGÄNGER	No pedestrians
KURZPARKZONE	Limited parking zone
LAWINENGEFAHR	Avalanche area
LINKS FAHREN	Keep left
LKW	Alternative route for heavy vehicles
NUR FÜR ANLIEGER	Access to residents only
PARKEN VERBOTEN	No parking
RECHTS FAHREN	Keep right
SCHLECHTE FAHRBAHN	Bad road surface
SCHULE	School
STEINSCHLAG	Falling rocks
STRASSENARBEITEN	Road works ahead (men working)
UMLEITUNG	Diversion (detour)
...VERBOTEN	No...
VORSICHT	Caution
WIRD EINGEFAHREN	Running-in (breaking-in) motor

FOR INTERNATIONAL ROAD SIGNS, see pages 160-161

Part B

Accidents

This section is confined to immediate aid. The legal problems of responsibility and settlement can be taken care of at a later stage. Your first concern will be for the injured.

Is anyone hurt?	**Ist jemand verletzt?**	ist **yay**mahnt fehr**lehtst**
Don't move.	**Bewegen Sie sich nicht.**	ber**vay**gern zee zikh nikht
It's all right. Don't worry.	**Es geht gut. Keine Sorge.**	ehss gayt goot. **kigh**ner **zor**ger
Where's the nearest telephone?	**Wo ist das nächste Telephon?**	voa ist dahss **nehkh**ster taylay**foan**
Can I use your telephone? There's been an accident.	**Kann ich Ihr Telephon benutzen? Es hat einen Unfall gegeben.**	kahn ikh eer taylay**foan** ber**nut**sern ehss haht **igh**nern **un**fahl ger**gay**bern
Call a doctor (an ambulance) immediately.	**Rufen Sie schnell einen Arzt (einen Krankenwagen).**	**roo**fern zee shnehl **igh**nern ahrtst (**igh**nern **krahngk**ernvargern)
There are people injured.	**Es hat Verletzte gegeben.**	ehss haht fehr**lehts**ter ger**gay**bern
Help me get them out of the car.	**Helfen Sie mir, sie aus dem Wagen zu holen.**	**hehl**fern zee meer zee owss daym **var**gern tsu **hoa**lern

Police—Exchange of information

Please call the police.	**Rufen Sie bitte die Polizei.**	**roo**fern zee **bit**ter dee poali**tsigh**
There's been an accident. It's about 2 km. from...	**Es ist ein Unfall passiert, ungefähr 2 Kilometer von...**	ehss ist ighn **un**fahl pah**sseert un**gerfair 2 killoam**may**terr fon
I'm on the Frankfurt–Cologne motorway (expressway), 25 km. from Cologne.	**Ich bin auf der Autobahn Frankfurt–Köln, 25 Kilometer von Köln.**	ikh bin owf derr **ow**toabarn **frahngk**foort–kurln 25 killoam**may**terr fon kurln
Here's my name and address.	**Hier ist mein Name und meine Adresse.**	heer ist mighn **nar**mer unt **migh**ner ah**dreh**sser

Would you mind acting as a witness?	**Würden Sie bitte als Zeuge auftreten?**	**vewr**dern zee **bi**tter ahlss **tsoy**ger **owf**traytern
I'd like an interpreter.	**Ich hätte gern einen Dolmetscher.**	ikh **heh**ter gehrn **igh**nern **dol**mehtsherr

Remember to put out a red warning triangle if the car is out of action or impeding traffic.

Breakdown

...and that's what we'll do with this section: break it down into four phases.

1. *On the road*
   You ask where the nearest garage is.
2. *At the garage*
   You tell the mechanic what's wrong.
3. *Finding the trouble*
   He tells you what he thinks is wrong.
4. *Getting it repaired*
   You tell him to repair it, and once that's over settle the account (or argue about it).

Phase 1—On the road

Where's the nearest garage?	**Wo ist die nächste Reparaturwerkstatt?**	voa ist dee **nehkh**ster raypahrah**toor**vehrkshtaht
Excuse me. My car has broken down. May I use your phone?	**Entschuldigung, mein Wagen hat eine Panne. Darf ich Ihr Telephon benutzen?**	ehnt**shul**digung mighn **var**gern haht **igh**ner **pah**ner. dahrf ikh eer taylay**foan** bernutsern
What's the telephone number of the nearest garage?	**Welche Telephonnummer hat die nächste Reparaturwerkstatt?**	**vehl**kher taylay**foan**nummerr haht dee **nehkh**ster raypahrah**toor**vehrkshtaht
I've had a breakdown at...	**Ich habe eine Panne in...**	ikh **har**ber **igh**ner **pah**ner in

Can you send a mechanic?	**Können Sie einen Mechaniker schicken?**	**kur**nern zee **igh**nern meh**khan**ikkerr **shik**kern
Can you send a truck to tow my car?	**Können Sie einen Abschleppwagen schicken?**	**kur**nern zee **igh**nern **ahp**shlehpvargern **shik**kern
How long will you be?	**Wie lange dauert es?**	vee **lang**er **dow**errt ehss

Phase 2—At the garage

Can you help me?	**Können Sie mir helfen?**	**kur**nern zee meer **hehl**fern
I don't know what's wrong with it.	**Ich weiß nicht, was mit dem Wagen los ist.**	ikh vighss nikht vahss mit daym **var**gern loass ist
I think there's something wrong with the...	**Ich glaube, ... ist/sind nicht in Ordnung.**	ikh **glow**ber ... ist/zint nikht in **ort**nung
battery	**die Batterie**	dee bahteh**ree**
brakes	**die Bremsen**	dee **brehm**zern
bulbs	**die Glühbirnen**	dee **glew**birnern
carburettor	**der Vergaser**	derr fehr**gar**zerr
clutch	**die Kupplung**	dee **kup**lung
cooling system	**die Kühlung**	dee **kew**lung
contact	**der Kontakt**	derr kon**tahkt**
dipswitch (dimmer)	**der Abblendschalter**	derr **ahp**blehntshahlterr
dynamo	**die Lichtmaschine**	dee **likht**mahsheener
electrical system	**die elektrische Anlage**	dee eh**lehk**trisher **ahn**larger
engine	**der Motor**	derr **moa**toar
exhaust pipe	**das Auspuffrohr**	dahss **ows**pufroar
fan	**der Ventilator**	derr vehntil**lar**toar
filter	**der Filter**	derr **fil**terr
fuel pump	**die Benzinpumpe**	dee behn**tseen**pumper
fuel tank	**der Benzintank**	derr behn**tseen**tahnk
gear shift	**die Gangschaltung**	dee **gahng**shahltung
generator	**die Lichtmaschine**	dee **likht**mahsheener
hand brake	**die Handbremse**	dee **hahnt**brehmzer
headlights	**die Scheinwerfer**	dee **shighn**vehrferr
heating	**die Heizung**	dee **high**tsung
horn	**die Hupe**	dee **hoo**per
ignition system	**die Zündung**	dee **tsewn**dung
indicator	**der Blinker**	derr **blin**kerr

CAR—REPAIRS

lights	**die Beleuchtung**	dee ber**loykh**tung
back-up lights	**Rückfahrleuchten**	**rewk**farrloykhtern
brake lights	**Bremsleuchten**	**brehms**loykhtern
rear lights	**Schlußleuchten**	**shlus**loykhtern
reversing lights	**Rückfahrleuchten**	**rewk**farrloykhtern
tail lights	**Schlußleuchten**	**shlus**loykhtern
lines	**die Leitungen**	dee **ligh**tungern
lining and covering	**der Bremsbelag und Bremsschutz**	derr **brehms**berlarg unt **brehms**shuts
lubrication system	**das Schmiersystem**	dahss **shmeer**sistaym
parking brake	**die Handbremse**	dee **hahnt**brehmzer
radiator	**der Kühler**	derr **kew**lerr
seat	**der Sitz**	derr zits
sliding roof	**das Schiebedach**	dahss **shee**berdahkh
sparking plugs	**die Zündkerzen**	dee **tsewnt**kehrtsern
speedometer	**der Tachometer**	derr tahkhom**may**terr
starter	**der Anlasser**	derr **ahn**lahsserr
steering	**die Lenkung**	dee **lehng**kung
suspension	**die Federung**	dee **fay**derrung
transmission	**das Getriebe**	dahss ger**tree**ber
turn signal	**der Blinker**	derr **bling**kerr
wheels	**die Räder**	dee **rai**derr
wipers	**die Scheibenwischer**	dee **shigh**bernvisherr

LEFT	RIGHT	FRONT	BACK
LINKS	**RECHTS**	**VORNE**	**HINTEN**
(links)	(rehkhts)	(**for**ner)	(**hin**tern)

It's...	**Es...**	ehss
bad	**ist schadhaft**	ist **shard**haft
blowing	**schließt nicht**	shleest nikht
blown	**ist durchgebrannt**	ist **doorkh**gerbrahnt
broken	**ist gebrochen**	ist ger**bro**khern
burnt	**ist verbrannt**	ist fehr**brahnt**
cracked	**ist gesprungen**	ist ger**shprung**ern
defective	**ist defekt**	ist day**fehkt**
disconnected	**ist losgelöst**	ist **los**gerlurst
dry	**ist trocken**	ist **trok**kern
frozen	**ist eingefroren**	ist **ighn**gerfroarern
jammed	**ist blockiert**	ist blok**keert**
knocking	**klopft**	klopft
leaking	**ist undicht**	ist **un**dikht
loose	**ist lose**	ist **loa**zer

misfiring	**gibt Fehlzündungen**	gipt **fayl**tsewndungern
noisy	**ist zu laut**	ist tsu lowt
not working	**funktioniert nicht**	funktsion**neert** nikht
overheating	**ist überhitzt**	ist ewberr**hitst**
short-circuiting	**hat Kurzschluß**	hat **koorts**shluss
slack	**ist locker**	ist **lok**kerr
slipping	**rutscht**	rucht
stuck	**ist verklemmt**	ist fehr**klehmt**
vibrating	**vibriert**	vi**breert**
weak	**ist zu schwach**	ist tsu shvahkh
worn	**ist verschlissen**	ist fehr**shlis**sern
The car won't start.	**Der Wagen springt nicht an.**	derr **var**gern shpringt nikht ahn
It's locked and the keys are inside.	**Er ist abgeschlossen und die Schlüssel sind drinnen.**	err ist **ahp**gershlossern unt dee **shlew**sserl zint **drin**nern
The fan belt is too slack.	**Der Keilriemen ist zu schlaff.**	derr **kighl**reemern ist tsu shlahf
The radiator is leaking.	**Der Kühler ist undicht.**	derr **kew**lerr ist **un**dikht
I want maintenance and lubrication service.	**Ich möchte Wartungs- und Schmierdienst.**	ikh **murkh**ter **vahr**tungs-unt **shmeer**deenst
The idling needs adjusting.	**Der Leerlauf muß eingestellt werden.**	derr **layr**lowf muss **ighn**gershtehlt **vayr**dern
The clutch engages too quickly.	**Die Kupplung greift zu schnell.**	dee **kup**lung grighft tsu shnehl
The steering wheel's vibrating.	**Das Steuerrad vibriert.**	dahss **shtoy**errrard vi**breert**
The wipers are smearing.	**Die Scheiben-wischer schmieren.**	dee **shigh**bernvisherr **shmee**rern
The pneumatic suspension is weak.	**Die Luftdruck-federung ist zu weich.**	dee **luft**drukfayderrung ist tsu vighkh

Now that you've explained what's wrong, you'll want to know how long it'll take to repair it and make your arrangements accordingly.

How long will it take to repair?	**Wie lange dauert die Reparatur?**	vee **lahn**ger **dow**errt dee raypahrah**toor**

CAR—REPAIRS

How long will it take to find out what's wrong?	**Wie lange brauchen Sie, um den Fehler zu finden?**	vee **lahng**er **brow**khern zee um dayn **fay**lerr tsu **fin**dern
Suppose I come back in half an hour?	**Kann ich in einer halben Stunde zurückkommen?**	kahn ikh in **igh**nerr **hahl**bern **shtun**der tsoo**rewk**kommern
Can you give me a lift into town?	**Können Sie mich in die Stadt fahren?**	**kur**nern zee mikh in dee shtaht **far**rern
Is there a place to stay nearby?	**Kann man hier in der Nähe übernachten?**	kahn mahn heer in derr naier ewberr**nahkh**tern

Phase 3—Finding the trouble

It's up to the mechanic either to find the trouble or to repair it. All you have to do is hand him the book and point to the text in German below.

Bitte sehen Sie in dieser alphabetisch geordneten Liste nach, und weisen Sie auf das, was am Wagen nicht in Ordnung ist. Wenn Ihr Kunde wissen will, was damit los ist, zeigen Sie ihm den zutreffenden Ausdruck in der nächsten Liste (gebrochen, Kurzschluß usw.).*

Abblendschalter	dipswitch (dimmer switch)
automatisches Getriebe	automatic transmission
Batterie	battery
Batterieflüssigkeit	battery liquid
Batteriezellen	battery cells
Belag	lining
Benzinfilter	fuel filter
Benzinpumpe	fuel pump
Bremsbacken	brake shoes
Bremse	brake
Bremstrommel	brake drum
destilliertes Wasser	distilled water
Druckfedern	pressure springs
Einspritzpumpe	injection pump

* Please look at the following alphabetical list and point to the defective item. If your customer wants to know what's wrong with it, pick the applicable term from the next list (broken, short-circuited, etc.)

Elektrische Anlage	electrical system
Federn	springs
Federung	suspension
Filter	filter
Gangschaltung	gear shift
Gelenk	joint
Getriebe	gearbox (transmission)
Getriebegehäuse	transmission case
Hauptlager	main bearings
Kabel	cable
Kardangelenk	universal joint
Kolben	piston
Kolbenringe	piston rings
Kondensator	condensor
Kontakt	contact
Kühler	radiator
Kühlung	cooling system
Kupplung	clutch
Kupplungspedal	clutch pedal
Kupplungsscheibe	clutch plate
Kurbelwelle	crankshaft
Kurbelwellengehäuse	crankcase
Lenkgehäuse	steering box
Lenksäule	steering column
Lichtmaschine	dynamo (generator)
Luftdruckfederung	pneumatic suspension
Luftfilter	air filter
Membrane	diaphragm
Motor	engine
Motorblock	block
Nockenwelle	camshaft
Ölfilter	oil filter
Ölpumpe	oil pump
Pumpe	pump
Räder	wheels
Schmierfett	grease
Schwimmer	float
Spurstangenenden	track rod ends
Stabilisator	stabilizer
Starter	starter motor
Steuerung	steering
Stoßdämpfer	shock-absorber
Stößel	tappets
Stoßstange	fender (bumper)
Thermostat	thermostat
Ventil	valve
Ventilator	fan

Ventilfeder	valve spring
Vergaser	carburettor
Verteiler	distributor
Verteilerfinger	distributor leads
Wasserpumpe	water pump
Welle	shaft
Zähne	teeth
Zahnstangengetriebe	rack and pinion
Zündkerzen	sparking plugs
Zündkerzenkabel	sparking-plug leads
Zündspule	ignition coil
Zylinder	cylinder
Zylinderkopf	cylinder head
Zylinderkopfdichtung	cylinder-head gasket

Die Ausdrücke in der folgenden Liste helfen Ihnen, zu erklären, was nicht in Ordnung ist und wie man den Schaden beheben kann.*

abgenutzt	worn
anziehen	to tighten
aufladen	to charge
ausbauen	to strip down
auswechseln	to change
auswuchten	to balance
blockiert	jammed
defekt	defective
durchgebrannt	blown
einschleifen	to grind in
entlüften	to bleed
ersetzen	to replace
Fehlzündung haben	misfiring
gefroren	frozen
gesprungen	cracked
(zu) hoch	(too) high
kaputt	broken
klopft	knocking
(zu) kurz	(too) short
Kurzschluß haben	short-circuited
lockern	to loosen
lose	loose
losgelöst	disconnected
nachstellen	to adjust

* The following list contains words which describe what's wrong as well as what may need to be done.

neubelegen	to reline
(zu) niedrig	(too) low
reinigen	to clean
rutscht	slipping
(zu) schlaff	(too) slack
schließt nicht	blowing
(zu) schnell	(too) quick
(zu) schwach	(too) weak
Spiel haben	play
trocken	dry
überhitzt	overheating
undicht	leaking
verbogen	warped
verbrannt	burnt
verklemmt	stuck
verrostet	corroded
verschmutzt	dirty
vibriert	vibrating

Phase 4—Getting it repaired

Have you found the trouble?	**Haben Sie den Fehler gefunden?**	**har**bern zee dayn **fay**lerr ger**fun**dern

Now that you know what's wrong, or at least have some idea, you'll want to find out...

Is that serious?	**Ist das schlimm?**	ist dahss shlim
Can you repair it?	**Können Sie es reparieren?**	**kur**nern zee ehss raypah**reer**ern
Can you do it now?	**Können Sie es sofort reparieren?**	**kur**nern zee ehss zoa**fort** raypah**reer**ern
What's it going to cost?	**Was wird es kosten?**	vahss veert ehss **kos**tern
Do you have the necessary spare parts?	**Haben Sie die nötigen Ersatzteile?**	**har**bern zee dee **nur**tiggern ehr**zahts**tighler

What if he says "no"?

Why can't you do it?	**Warum können Sie es nicht reparieren?**	vah**rum kur**nern zee ehss nikht raypah**reer**ern
Is it essential to have that part?	**Geht es nicht ohne dieses Ersatzteil?**	gayt ehss nikht **oa**ner **dee**zerss ehr**zahts**tighl

How long is it going to take to get the spare parts?	**Wie lange brauchen Sie für die Beschaffung der Ersatzteile?**	vee **lahng**er **brow**khern zee fewr dee ber**shah**fung derr ehr**zahts**tighler
Where's the nearest garage that can repair it?	**Wo ist die nächste Werkstatt, die das reparieren kann?**	voa ist dee **nehkh**ster **vehrk**shtaht dee dahss raypah**ree**rern kahn
Can you fix it so that I can get as far as...?	**Können Sie es so reparieren, dass ich noch bis...komme?**	**kur**nern zee ehss zoa raypah**ree**rern dahss ikh nokh biss ... **kom**mer

If you're really stuck, ask if you can leave the car at the garage. Contact an automobile association or hire another car.

Settling the bill

Is everything fixed?	**Ist der Schaden behoben?**	ist derr **shar**dern ber**hoa**bern
How much do I owe you?	**Was schulde ich Ihnen?**	vahss **shul**der ikh **ee**nern

The garage then presents you with the bill. If you're satisfied...

Will you take a traveller's cheque?	**Nehmen Sie Reiseschecks?**	**nay**mern zee **righ**zershehks
Thanks very much for your help.	**Vielen Dank für Ihre Hilfe.**	**fee**lern dahnk fewr **ee**rer **hil**fer
This is for you.	**Das ist für Sie.**	dahss ist fewr zee

But you may feel that the workmanship is sloppy or that you're paying for work not done. Get the bill itemized. If necessary, get it translated before you pay.

I'd like to check the bill first. Will you itemize the work done?	**Ich möchte die Rechnung erst prüfen. Können Sie die Arbeit spezifizieren?**	ikh **murkh**ter dee **rehkh**nung ehrst **prew**fern. **kur**nern zee dee **ahr**bight shpehtsiffit**see**rern

If the garage still won't back down and you're sure you're right, get the help of a third party.

Some international road signs

No vehicles

No entry

No overtaking (passing)

Oncoming traffic has priority

Maximum speed limit

No parking

Caution

Intersection

Dangerous bend (curve)

Road narrows

Intersection with secondary road

Two-way traffic

Dangerous hill

Uneven road

Falling rocks

Give way (yield)

Main road, thoroughfare

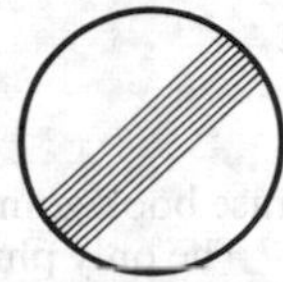

End of restriction

One-way traffic

Traffic goes this way

Roundabout (rotary)

Bicycles only

Pedestrians only

Minimum speed limit

Keep right (left if symbol reversed)

Parking

Hospital

Motorway (expressway)

Motor vehicles only

Filling station

No through road

Doctor

Frankly, how much use is a phrase book going to be to you in case of serious injury or illness? The only phrase you need in such an emergency is...

Get a doctor quickly!	**Rufen Sie schnell einen Arzt!**	**roo**fern zee shnehl **igh**nern ahrtst

But there are minor aches and pains, ailments and irritations that can upset the best-planned trip. Here we can help you and, perhaps, the doctor.

Some doctors will speak English well; others will know enough for your needs. But suppose there's something the doctor can't explain because of language difficulties? We've thought of that. As you'll see, this section has been arranged to enable you and the doctor to communicate. From pages 165 to 171, you find your part of the dialogue on the upper half of each page—the doctor's is on the lower half.

The whole section has been divided into three parts: illness, wounds, nervous tension. Page 171 is concerned with prescriptions and fees.

General

I need a doctor quickly.	**Ich brauche schnell einen Arzt.**	ikh **brow**kher shnehl **igh**nern ahrtst
Can you get me a doctor?	**Können Sie einen Arzt für mich finden?**	**kur**nern zee **igh**nern ahrtst fewr mikh **fin**dern
Is there a doctor here?	**Gibt es hier einen Arzt?**	gipt ehss heer **igh**nern ahrtst
Please telephone for a doctor immediately.	**Bitte rufen Sie sofort einen Arzt an.**	**bit**ter **roo**fern zee zoa**fort** **igh**nern ahrtst ahn
Where's there a doctor who speaks English?	**Wo gibt es einen Arzt, der Englisch spricht?**	voa gipt ehss **igh**nern ahrtst derr **ehng**lish shprikht

Where's the surgery (doctor's office)?	**Wo ist die Arztpraxis?**	voa ist dee **ahrtst**prahksiss
What are the surgery (office) hours?	**Wann sind die Sprechstunden?**	vahn zint dee **shprekh**shtundern
Could the doctor come to see me here?	**Könnte der Arzt mich hier behandeln?**	**kurn**ter derr ahrtst mikh heer berhahnderln
What time can the doctor come?	**Wann kann der Arzt kommen?**	vahn kahn derr ahrtst **kom**mern

Symptoms

Use this section to tell the doctor what's wrong. Basically, what he'll require to know is:

What? (ache, pain, bruise, etc.)
Where? (arm, stomach, etc.)
How long? (have you had the trouble)

Before you visit the doctor, find out the answers to these questions by glancing through the pages that follow. In this way, you'll save time.

Parts of the body

ankle	**der Knöchel**	derr **knur**kherl
appendix	**der Blinddarm**	derr **blint**dahrm
arm	**der Arm**	derr ahrm
artery	**die Arterie**	dee ahr**tay**rier
back	**der Rücken**	derr **rew**kern
bladder	**die Blase**	dee **blar**zer
blood	**das Blut**	dahss bloot
bone	**der Knochen**	derr **kno**khern
bowels	**der Darm**	derr dahrm
breast	**die Brust**	dee brust
cheek	**die Backe**	dee **bah**ker
chest	**der Brustkorb**	derr **brust**korp
chin	**das Kinn**	dahss kin
collar-bone	**das Schlüsselbein**	dahss **shlew**sserlbighn
ear	**das Ohr**	dahss oar
elbow	**der Ellbogen**	derr **ehl**boagern
eye	**das Auge**	dahss **ow**ger
face	**das Gesicht**	dahss ger**zikht**
finger	**der Finger**	derr **fing**err

foot	**der Fuß**	derr fooss
forehead	**die Stirn**	dee shteern
gland	**die Drüse**	dee **drew**zer
hair	**das Haar**	dahss harr
hand	**die Hand**	dee hahnt
head	**der Kopf**	derr kopf
heart	**das Herz**	dahss hehrts
heel	**die Ferse**	dee **fehr**zer
hip	**die Hüfte**	dee **hewf**ter
intestines	**die Eingeweide**	dee **ighn**gervighder
jaw	**der Kiefer**	derr **kee**ferr
joint	**das Gelenk**	dahss ger**lehngk**
kidney	**die Niere**	dee **nee**rer
knee	**das Knie**	dahss knee
knee cap	**die Kniescheibe**	dee **knee**shighber
leg	**das Bein**	dahss bighn
lip	**die Lippe**	dee **lip**per
liver	**die Leber**	dee **lay**berr
lung	**die Lunge**	dee **lung**er
mouth	**der Mund**	derr munt
muscle	**der Muskel**	derr **mus**kerl
neck	**der Hals**	derr hahls
nerve	**der Nerv**	derr nehrf
nervous system	**das Nervensystem**	dahss **nehr**fernzewstaym
nose	**die Nase**	dee **nar**zer
rib	**die Rippe**	dee **rip**per
shoulder	**die Schulter**	dee **shul**terr
skin	**die Haut**	dee howt
spine	**die Wirbelsäule**	dee **veer**berlzoyler
stomach	**der Magen**	derr **mar**gern
tendon	**die Sehne**	dee **zay**ner
thigh	**der Schenkel**	derr **shehng**kerl
throat	**der Hals**	derr hahls
thumb	**der Daumen**	derr **dow**mern
toe	**die Zehe**	dee **tsay**er
tongue	**die Zunge**	dee **tsung**er
tonsils	**die Mandeln**	dee **mahn**derln
urine	**der Urin**	derr oo**reen**
vein	**die Vene**	dee **vay**ner
wrist	**das Handgelenk**	dahss **hahnt**gerlehnk

the left.../on the left side
der/die/das linke.../links
(der/dee/dahss **ling**ker/links)

the right.../on the right side
der/die/das rechte.../rechts
(derr/dee/dahss **rehkh**ter/ rehkhts)

PATIENT

Part 1—Illness

I'm not feeling well.	**Ich fühle mich nicht wohl.**	ikh **few**ler mikh nikht voal
I'm ill.	**Ich bin krank.**	ikh bin krahngk
I've got a pain here.	**Ich habe hier Schmerzen.**	ikh **har**ber heer **shmehr**tsern
His / Her ... hurts.	**Sein/Ihr ... tut weh.**	zighn / eer ... toot vay
I've got (a) ...	**Ich habe ...**	ikh **har**ber
backache	**Rückenschmerzen**	**rew**kernshmehrtsern
fever	**Fieber**	**fee**berr
headache	**Kopfschmerzen**	**kopf**shmehrtsern
sore throat	**Halsschmerzen**	**hahls**shmehrtsern
travel sickness	**Reisekrankheit**	**righ**zerkrahngk-hight
I'm constipated.	**Ich habe Verstopfung.**	ikh **har**ber fehr**shto**pfung
I've been vomiting.	**Ich habe mich übergeben.**	ikh **har**ber mikh ewberr**gay**bern

---

DOCTOR

1—Krankheit

Was fehlt Ihnen?	What's the trouble?
Wo haben Sie Schmerzen?	Where does it hurt?
Wie lange haben Sie diese Schmerzen schon?	How long have you had this pain?
Wie lange fühlen Sie sich schon so?	How long have you been feeling like this?
Streifen Sie den Ärmel hoch.	Roll up your sleeve.
Bitte machen Sie den Oberkörper frei.	Please undress down to the waist.
Ziehen Sie bitte Hose und Unterhose aus.	Please remove your trousers and underpants.

PATIENT

I feel faint/I feel dizzy.	**Ich fühle mich schwach/Mir ist schwindlig.**	ikh **few**ler mikh shvahkh/meer ist **shvind**likh
I'm nauseous.	**Mir ist übel.**	meer ist **ew**berl
I feel shivery.	**Mich fröstelt.**	mikh **frur**sterlt
I've/He's got/She's got (a/an)...	**Ich habe/Er hat/Sie hat...**	ikh **har**ber/ehr haht/ zee haht
abscess	**einen Abszeß**	**igh**nern ahps**tsehss**
asthma	**Asthma**	**ahst**mah
boil	**einen Furunkel**	**igh**nern foo**rung**kerl
cold	**eine Erkältung**	**igh**ner ehr**kehl**tung
constipation	**Verstopfung**	fehr**shto**pfung
cramps	**Krämpfe**	**kreh**mpfer
diarrhoea	**Durchfall**	**doorkh**fahl
fever	**Fieber**	**fee**berr
haemorrhoids	**Hämorrhoiden**	hehmoaroa**ee**dern
hay fever	**Heufieber**	**hoy**feeberr
hernia	**einen Bruch**	**igh**nern brukh

DOCTOR

Legen Sie sich bitte hierhin.	Please lie down over here.
Machen Sie den Mund auf.	Open your mouth.
Tief atmen, bitte.	Breathe deeply.
Husten Sie bitte.	Cough, please.
Ich werde Ihre Temperatur messen.	I'll take your temperature.
Ich werde Ihren Blutdruck messen.	I'm going to take your blood pressure.
Haben Sie das zum ersten Mal?	Is it the first time you've had this?
Ich gebe Ihnen eine Spritze.	I'll give you an injection.
Ich möchte eine Urinprobe (Stuhlprobe) von Ihnen.	I want a specimen of your urine (stools).

PATIENT

indigestion	**eine Magen-verstimmung**	**igh**ner **mar**gern-fehrshtimmung
inflammation of...	**eine ... entzündung**	**igh**ner ... ehnt**tsewn**dung
influenza	**Grippe**	**grip**per
morning sickness	**morgendliches Erbrechen**	**mor**gerntlikherss ehr**breh**khern
rheumatism	**Rheuma**	**roy**mah
stiff neck	**einen steifen Nacken**	**igh**nern **shtigh**fern **nah**kern
sunburn	**Sonnenbrand**	**zon**nernbrahnt
sunstroke	**einen Sonnenstich**	**igh**nern **zon**nernshtikh
tonsillitis	**Mandelentzündung**	**mahn**derlehnttsewndung
ulcer	**ein Geschwür**	ighn ger**shvewr**
whooping cough	**Keuchhusten**	**koykh**hoostern
It's nothing serious, I hope?	**Es ist hoffentlich nichts Ernstes?**	ehss ist **hof**ferntlikh nikhts **ehrn**sterss
I'd like you to prescribe some medicine for me.	**Ich möchte, daß Sie mir ein Medikament verschreiben.**	Ikh **murkh**ter dahss zee meer ighn mehdikkah**mehnt** fehr**shrigh**bern

---

DOCTOR

Sie brauchen sich keine Sorgen zu machen.	It's nothing to worry about.
Sie müssen ... Tage im Bett bleiben.	You must stay in bed for... days.
Sie haben ...	You've got (a/an)....
eine Erkältung/Grippe	cold/influenza
eine Lungenentzündung	pneumonia
Arthritis	arthritis
Blinddarmentzündung	appendicitis
Sie rauchen zuviel.	You're smoking too much.
Sie trinken zuviel.	You're drinking too much.
Sie müssen zu einer General-untersuchung ins Krankenhaus.	I want you to go to hospital for a general check-up.
Ich werde Ihnen ein Antibiotikum verschreiben.	I'll prescribe an antibiotic.

PATIENT

I'm a diabetic.	**Ich bin Diabetiker.**	ikh bin diah**bay**tikkerr
I've a cardiac condition.	**Ich habe ein Herzleiden.**	ikh **har**ber ighn **hehrts**lighdern
I had a heart attack in…	**Ich hatte einen Herzanfall im…**	ikh **hah**ter **igh**nern **hehrts**ahnfahl im
I'm allergic to…	**Ich bin gegen … allergisch.**	ikh bin **gay**gern … ah**lehr**gish
This is my usual medicine.	**Gewöhnlich nehme ich dieses Medikament.**	ger**vurn**likh **nay**mer ikh **dee**zerss maydikah**mehnt**
I need this medicine.	**Ich brauche dieses Medikament.**	**ikh brow**kher **deezerss** maydikah**mehnt**
I'm expecting a baby.	**Ich erwarte ein Baby.**	ikh ehr**vahr**ter ighn **bay**bee
Can I travel?	**Kann ich reisen?**	kahn ikh **righ**zern

DOCTOR

Welche Dosis Insulin nehmen Sie?	What dose of insulin are you taking?
Einspritzung oder Tabletten?	Injection or oral?
Wie sind Sie behandelt worden?	What treatment have you been having?
Welches Medikament haben Sie genommen?	What medicine have you been taking?
Sie haben einen (leichten) Herzanfall gehabt.	You've had a (slight) heart attack.
…führen wir in Deutschland nicht. Dies ist ein ähnliches Mittel.	We don't use…in Germany. This is very similar.
Wann erwarten Sie das Baby?	When is the baby due?
Sie können nicht reisen bis…	You can't travel until…

PATIENT

Part 2—Wounds

I've got a/an... Could you have a look at it?	**Ich habe... Bitte sehen Sie es mal an.**	ikh **har**ber ... **bit**ter **zay**ern zee ehss marl ahn
blister	**eine Blase**	ighner **blar**zer
boil	**einen Furunkel**	ighnern foo**rung**kerl
bruise	**eine Quetschung**	ighner **kveht**shung
burn	**eine Brandwunde**	ighner **brahnt**vunder
cut	**eine Schnittwunde**	ighner **shnit**vunder
graze	**eine Abschürfung**	ighner **ahp**shewrfung
insect bite	**einen Insektenstich**	ighnern in**zehk**ternshtikh
lump	**eine Beule**	ighner **boy**ler
rash	**einen Ausschlag**	ighnern **ows**shlarg
sting	**einen Stich**	ighnern shtikh
swelling	**eine Schwellung**	ighner **shveh**lung
wound	**eine Wunde**	ighner **vun**der
I can't move... It hurts.	**Ich kann... nicht bewegen. Es schmerzt.**	ikh kahn ... nikht ber**vay**gern. ehss shmehrtst

---

DOCTOR

2—Wunden

Es ist (nicht) infiziert.	It is (not) infected.
Sie haben einen Bandscheibenvorfall.	You've got a slipped disc.
Sie müssen geröntgt werden.	You'll need an X-ray.
Es ist...	It's...
gebrochen/verstaucht verrenkt/gerissen	broken/sprained dislocated/torn
Sie haben eine Muskelzerrung.	You've pulled a muscle.
Ich gebe Ihnen ein Antiseptikum. Es ist nichts Ernstes.	I'll give you an antiseptic. It's not serious.
In... Tagen möchte ich Sie wieder sehen.	I want you to come and see me in ... days' time.

PATIENT

Part 3—Nervous tension

I'm in a nervous state.	**Ich bin übernervös.**	ikh bin **ew**berrnehrvurss
I'm feeling depressed.	**Ich habe Depressionen.**	ikh **har**ber dayprehs**sioa**nern
I want some sleeping pills.	**Ich brauche Schlaftabletten.**	ikh brow**kher** **shlarf**tahblehtern
I can't eat/I can't sleep.	**Ich kann nicht essen/Ich kann nicht schlafen.**	ikh kahn nikht **eh**ssern/ikh kahn nikht **shlar**fern
I'm having nightmares.	**Ich habe Alpträume.**	ikh **har**ber **ahlp**troymer
Can you prescribe a...?	**Können Sie mir ein ...verschreiben?**	**kur**nern zee meer ighn... fehr**shrigh**bern
sedative	**Beruhigungsmittel**	ber**roo**iggungsmitterl
anti-depressant	**Mittel gegen Depressionen**	**mit**terl **gay**gern dayprehs**sioa**nern

---

DOCTOR

3—Unruhe/Nervosität

Sie leiden unter nervöser Spannung.	You're suffering from nervous tension.
Sie brauchen Ruhe.	You need a rest.
Welche Tabletten haben Sie genommen?	What pills have you been taking?
Wie viele pro Tag?	How many a day?
Wie lange fühlen Sie sich schon so?	How long have you been feeling like this?
Ich verschreibe Ihnen Tabletten.	I'll prescribe some pills.
Ich gebe Ihnen ein Beruhigungsmittel.	I'll give you a sedative.

PATIENT

Prescriptions and dosage

What kind of medicine is this?	**Was für ein Medikament ist das?**	vahss fewr ighn maydikah**mehnt** ist dahss
How many times a day should I take it?	**Wie oft am Tag muß ich es nehmen?**	vee oft ahm targ muss ikh ehss **nay**mern
Must I swallow them whole?	**Muß ich sie ganz schlucken?**	muss ikh zee gahnts **shluk**kern

Fee

How much do I owe you?	**Wieviel bin ich Ihnen schuldig?**	vee**feel** bin ikh **ee**nern **shul**dikh
Do I pay you now or will you send me your bill?	**Soll ich gleich bezahlen oder schicken Sie mir die Rechnung?**	zol ikh glighkh ber**tsar**lern **oa**der **shik**kern zee meer dee **rehkh**nung
Thanks for your help, Doctor.	**Vielen Dank für Ihre Hilfe, Herr Doktor.**	**fee**lern dahnk fewr **ee**rer **hil**fer hehr **dok**toar

---

DOCTOR

Rezept und Dosis

Nehmen Sie von dieser Medizin ...Teelöffel alle...Stunden.	Take...teaspoons of this medicine every...hours.
Nehmen Sie...Tabletten mit einem Glas Wasser...	Take...pills with a glass of water...
...mal täglich	... times a day
vor jeder Mahlzeit	before each meal
nach jeder Mahlzeit	after each meal
morgens	in the mornings
abends	at night

Honorar

Das macht...Mark, bitte.	That's...marks, please.
Bitte zahlen Sie gleich jetzt.	Please pay me now.
Ich schicke Ihnen die Rechnung.	I'll send you a bill.

FOR NUMBERS, see page 175

Dentist

Can you recommend a good dentist?	**Können Sie einen guten Zahnarzt empfehlen?**	**kur**nern zee **igh**nern **goo**tern **tsarn**ahrtst ehm**pfay**lern
Can I make an (urgent) appointment to see Dr....?	**Kann ich einen (dringenden) Termin bei Herrn Dr.... ausmachen?**	kahn ikh **igh**nern (**dring**erndern) tehr**meen** bigh hehrn **dok**toar ... **ows**mahkhern
I've a toothache.	**Ich habe Zahnschmerzen.**	ikh **har**ber **tsarn**shmehrtsern
I've an abscess.	**Ich habe einen Abszeß.**	ikh **har**ber **igh**nern ahps**tsehss**
This tooth hurts.	**Dieser Zahn schmerzt.**	**dee**zerr tsarn shmehrtst
at the top	**oben**	**oa**bern
at the bottom	**unten**	**un**tern
in the front	**vorne**	**for**ner
at the back	**hinten**	**hin**tern
Can you fix it temporarily?	**Können Sie ihn provisorisch behandeln?**	**kur**nern zee een provvi**zoa**rish ber**hahn**derln
I don't want it extracted.	**Ich möchte ihn nicht ziehen lassen.**	ikh **murkh**ter een nikht **tsee**ern **lah**ssern
I've lost a filling.	**Ich habe eine Füllung verloren.**	ikh **har**ber **igh**ner **few**lung fehr**loa**rern
The gum is very sore.	**Das Zahnfleisch ist wund.**	dahss **tsarn**flighsh ist vunt
The gum is bleeding.	**Das Zahnfleisch blutet.**	dahss **tsarn**flighsh **bloo**tert

Dentures

I've broken this denture.	**Mein Gebiß ist zerbrochen.**	mighn ger**biss** ist tsehr**bro**khern
Can you repair this denture?	**Können Sie das Gebiß reparieren?**	**kur**nern zee dahss ger**biss** raypah**ree**rern
When will it be ready?	**Wann ist es fertig?**	vahn ist ehss **fehr**tikh

DENTIST

Optician

I've broken my glasses.	**Meine Brille ist zerbrochen.**	**migh**ner **bril**ler ist tsehr**brok**hern
Can you repair them for me?	**Können Sie sie reparieren?**	**kur**nern zee zee raypah**ree**rern
When will they be ready?	**Wann ist sie fertig?**	vahn ist zee **fehr**tikh
Can you change the lenses?	**Können Sie die Gläser auswechseln?**	**kur**nern zee dee **glai**zerr **ows**vehkserln
I want tinted lenses.	**Ich möchte getönte Gläser.**	ikh **murkh**ter ger**turn**ter **glai**zerr
I want some contact lenses.	**Ich möchte Kontaktlinsen.**	ikh **murkh**ter kon**tahkt**linzern
I'd like to buy a pair of binoculars.	**Ich hätte gern einen Feldstecher.**	ikh **heh**ter gehrn **igh**nern **fehlt**shtehkherr
I'd like to buy a pair of sun-glasses.	**Ich hätte gern eine Sonnenbrille.**	ikh **heh**ter gehrn **igh**ner **zon**nernbriller
How much do I owe you?	**Wieviel schulde ich Ihnen?**	vee**feel shul**der ikh **ee**nern
Do I pay you now or will you send me your bill?	**Soll ich jetzt bezahlen oder schicken Sie mir die Rechnung?**	zol ikh yehtst bert**sar**lern oader **shik**kern zee meer dee **rehkh**nung

FOR NUMBERS, see page 175

Reference section

Where do you come from?

Africa	**Afrika**	**ah**frikkah
Asia	**Asien**	**ar**ziern
Australia	**Australien**	ow**strar**liern
Austria	**Österreich**	**ur**sterrrighkh
Belgium	**Belgien**	**behl**giern
Canada	**Kanada**	**kah**nahdah
China	**China**	**khee**nah
Czechoslovakia	**Tschechoslowakei**	chehkhosloavah**kigh**
Denmark	**Dänemark**	**dai**nermahrk
England	**England**	**ehng**lahnt
Europe	**Europa**	oy**roa**pah
France	**Frankreich**	**frahngk**righkh
Federal Republic of Germany (West Germany)	**Bundesrepublik Deutschland**	**bun**dersrehpublik **doych**lahnt
German Democratic Republic (East Germany)	**Deutsche Demokratische Republik**	**doy**cher dehmo**krar**tisher rehpub**lik**
Germany	**Deutschland**	**doych**lahnt
Great Britain	**Großbritannien**	**groas**brittahniern
Holland	**Holland**	**hol**lahnt
Hungary	**Ungarn**	**un**gahrn
India	**Indien**	**in**diern
Ireland	**Irland**	**eer**lahnt
Italy	**Italien**	i**tar**liern
Japan	**Japan**	**yar**parn
Liechtenstein	**Liechtenstein**	**likh**ternshtighn
Luxemburg	**Luxemburg**	**luk**sermboorg
New Zealand	**Neuseeland**	noy**zay**lahnt
North America	**Nordamerika**	**nort**ahmayrikkah
Poland	**Polen**	**poa**lern
Scandinavia	**Skandinavien**	skahndin**nar**viern
Scotland	**Schottland**	**shot**lahnt
South Africa	**Südafrika**	**zewd**ahfrikkah
South America	**Südamerika**	**zewd**ahmayrikkah
Soviet Union	**Sowjetunion**	zov**yeht**unnioan
Spain	**Spanien**	**shpar**niern
Switzerland	**Schweiz**	shvights
United States	**Vereinigte Staaten**	feh**righ**nigter **shtar**tern
Wales	**Wales**	"Wales"
Yugoslavia	**Jugoslawien**	yuggos**lar**viern

Numbers

0	**null**	nul
1	**eins**	ighns
2	**zwei**	tsvigh
3	**drei**	drigh
4	**vier**	feer
5	**fünf**	fewnf
6	**sechs**	zehks
7	**sieben**	**zee**bern
8	**acht**	ahkht
9	**neun**	noyn
10	**zehn**	tsayn
11	**elf**	ehlf
12	**zwölf**	tsvurlf
13	**dreizehn**	**drigh**tsayn
14	**vierzehn**	**feer**tsayn
15	**fünfzehn**	**fewnf**tsayn
16	**sechzehn**	**zehkh**tsayn
17	**siebzehn**	**zeep**tsayn
18	**achtzehn**	**ahkh**tsayn
19	**neunzehn**	**noyn**tsayn
20	**zwanzig**	**tsvahn**tsikh
21	**einundzwanzig**	**ighn**unttsvahntsikh
22	**zweiundzwanzig**	**tsvigh**unttsvahntsikh
23	**dreiundzwanzig**	**drigh**unttsvahntsikh
24	**vierundzwanzig**	**feer**unttsvahntsikh
25	**fünfundzwanzig**	**fewnf**unttsvahntsikh
26	**sechsundzwanzig**	**zehks**unttsvahntsikh
27	**siebenundzwanzig**	**zee**bernunttsvahntsikh
28	**achtundzwanzig**	**ahkht**unttsvahntsikh
29	**neunundzwanzig**	**noyn**unttsvahntsikh
30	**dreißig**	**drigh**ssikh
31	**einunddreißig**	**ighn**untdrighssikh
32	**zweiunddreißig**	**tsvigh**untdrighssikh
33	**dreiunddreißig**	**drigh**untdrighssikh
40	**vierzig**	**feer**tsikh
41	**einundvierzig**	**ighn**untfeertsikh
42	**zweiundvierzig**	**tsvigh**untfeertsikh
43	**dreiundvierzig**	**drigh**untfeertsikh
50	**fünfzig**	**fewnf**tsikh
51	**einundfünfzig**	**ighn**untfewnftsikh
52	**zweiundfünfzig**	**tsvigh**untfewnftsikh
53	**dreiundfünfzig**	**drigh**untfewnftsikh
60	**sechzig**	**zehkh**tsikh
61	**einundsechzig**	**ighn**untzehkhtsikh

62	**zweiundsechzig**	**tsvigh**untzehkhtsikh
63	**dreiundsechzig**	**drigh**untzehkhtsikh
70	**siebzig**	**zeep**tsikh
71	**einundsiebzig**	**ighn**untzeeptsikh
72	**zweiundsiebzig**	**tsvigh**untzeeptsikh
73	**dreiundsiebzig**	**drigh**untzeeptsikh
80	**achtzig**	**ahkh**tsikh
81	**einundachtzig**	**ighn**untahkhtsikh
82	**zweiundachtzig**	**tsvigh**untahkhtsikh
83	**dreiundachtzig**	**drigh**untahkhtsikh
90	**neunzig**	**noyn**tsikh
91	**einundneunzig**	**ighn**untnoyntsikh
92	**zweiundneunzig**	**tsvigh**untnoyntsikh
93	**dreiundneunzig**	**drigh**untnoyntsikh
100	**(ein)hundert**	**(ighn) hun**derrt
101	**hunderteins**	**hun**derrtighnss
102	**hundertzwei**	**hun**derrttsvigh
110	**hundertzehn**	**hun**derrttsayn
120	**hundertzwanzig**	**hun**derrttsvahntsikh
130	**hundertdreißig**	**hun**derrtdrighssikh
140	**hundertvierzig**	**hun**derrtfeertsikh
150	**hundertfünfzig**	**hun**derrtfewnftsikh
160	**hundertsechzig**	**hun**derrtzehkhtsikh
170	**hundertsiebzig**	**hun**derrtzeeptsikh
180	**hundertachtzig**	**hun**derrtahkhtsikh
190	**hundertneunzig**	**hun**derrtnoyntsikh
200	**zweihundert**	**tsvigh**hunderrt
300	**dreihundert**	**drigh**hunderrt
400	**vierhundert**	**feer**hunderrt
500	**fünfhundert**	**fewnf**hunderrt
600	**sechshundert**	**zehks**hunderrt
700	**siebenhundert**	**zee**bernhunderrt
800	**achthundert**	**ahkht**hunderrt
900	**neunhundert**	**noyn**hunderrt
1000	**(ein)tausend**	(ighn) **tow**zernt
1100	**tausendeinhundert**	towzernt**ighn**hunderrt
1200	**tausendzweihundert**	towzernt**tsvigh**hunderrt
2000	**zweitausend**	**tsvigh**towzernt
5000	**fünftausend**	**fewnf**towzernt
10,000	**zehntausend**	**tsayn**towzernt
50,000	**fünfzigtausend**	**fewnf**tsikhtowzernt
100,000	**hunderttausend**	**hun**derrttowzernt
1,000,000	**eine Million**	**igh**ner mill**ioan**
1,000,000,000	**eine Milliarde**	**igh**ner milli**ahr**der

first	**erste**	**ehr**ster
second	**zweite**	**tsvigh**ter
third	**dritte**	**drit**ter
fourth	**vierte**	**feer**ter
fifth	**fünfte**	**fewnf**ter
sixth	**sechste**	**zehk**ster
seventh	**siebte**	**zeeb**ter
eighth	**achte**	**ahkh**ter
ninth	**neunte**	**noyn**ter
tenth	**zehnte**	**tsayn**ter
once	**einmal**	**ighn**marl
twice	**zweimal**	**tsvigh**marl
three times	**dreimal**	**drigh**marl
half a...	**ein halber...**	ighn **hahl**berr
half of...	**die Hälfte von...**	dee **hehlf**ter fon
half (adj.)	**halb**	hahlp
a quarter	**ein Viertel**	ighn **feer**terl
one third	**ein Drittel**	ighn **drit**terl
a pair of...	**ein Paar...**	ighn parr
a dozen	**ein Dutzend**	ighn **dut**sernd
1978	**neunzehnhundertachtundsiebzig** (noyntsaynhunderrt**ahkht**untzeeptsikh)	
1979	**neunzehnhundertneunundsiebzig** (noyntsaynhunderrt**noyn**untzeeptsikh)	
1980	**neunzehnhundertachtzig** (noyntsaynhunderrt**ahkh**tsikh)	
1981	**neunzehnhunderteinundachtzig** (noyntsaynhunderrt**ighn**untahkhtsikh)	
1982	**neunzehnhundertzweiundachtzig** (noyntsaynhunderrt**tsvigh**untahkhtsikh)	
1983	**neunzehnhundertdreiundachtzig** (noyntsaynhunderrt**drigh**untahkhtsikh)	

Time

viertel nach zwölf
(**fee**rterl narkh tsvurlf)

zwanzig nach eins
(**tsvahn**tsikh narkh ighns)

fünf vor halb drei
(fewnf foar hahlp drigh)

halb vier
(hahlp feer)

fünf nach halb fünf
(fewnf narkh hahlp fewnf)

zwanzig vor sechs
(**tsvahn**tsikh foar zehks)

viertel vor sieben
(**fee**rterl foar **zee**bern)

zehn vor acht
(tsayn foar ahkht)

fünf vor neun
(fewnf foar noyn)

zehn Uhr
(tsayn oor)

fünf nach elf
(fewnf narkh ehlf)

zehn nach zwölf
(tsayn narkh tsvurlf)

In ordinary conversation, time is expressed as above. However, official time uses a 24-hour clock which means that, after noon, hours are counted from 13 to 24. For instance, 13.15 would be 1.15 p.m. for us and 20.30 is 8.30 p.m. At midnight time returns to 0 so that 12.17 a.m. is written 0.17.

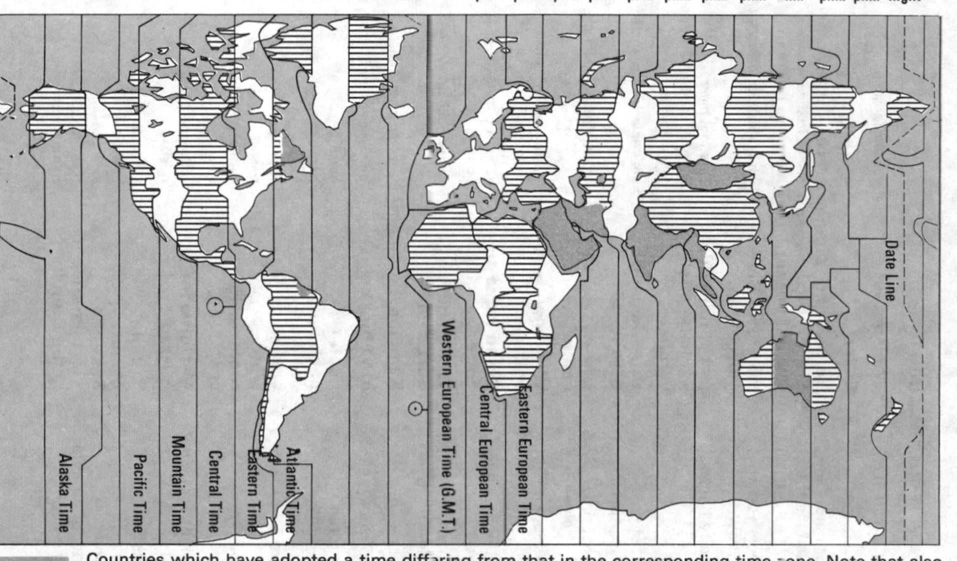

Countries which have adopted a time differing from that in the corresponding time zone. Note that also in the USSR, official time is one hour ahead of the time in each corresponding time zone. In summer, numerous countries advance time one hour ahead of standard time.

Have you got the time?

What time is it?	**Wie spät ist es?**	vee shpait ist ehss
It's...	**Es ist...**	ehss ist
Excuse me. Can you tell me the time?	**Verzeihung. Können Sie mir bitte sagen, wie spät es ist?**	fehr**tsigh**ung. **kur**nern zee meer **bit**ter **zar**gern vee shpait ehss ist
I'll meet you at... tomorrow.	**Ich treffe Sie morgen um...**	ikh **treh**fer zee **mor**gern um
I'm sorry I'm late.	**Es tut mir leid, ich habe mich verspätet.**	ehss toot meer light ikh **har**ber mikh fehr**shpai**tert
At what time does... open?	**Um wieviel Uhr öffnet...?**	um **vee**feel oor **urf**nert
At what time does... close?	**Um wieviel Uhr schließt...?**	um **vee**feel oor shleest
How long will it last?	**Wie lange wird es dauern?**	vee **lan**ger veert ehss **dow**errn
What time will it end?	**Wann ist es zu Ende?**	vahn ist ehss tsu **ehn**der
At what time should I be there?	**Wann soll ich dort sein?**	vahn zol ikh dort zighn
Can I come...?	**Kann ich...kommen?**	kahn ikh ... **kom**mern
at 8 o'clock/at 2:30	**um 8/um halb 3**	um 8/um hahlp 3
after (prep.)	**nach**	narkh
afterwards	**nachher**	**narkh**hayr
before (prep.)	**vor**	foar
before	**vorher**	**foar**hayr
early	**früh**	frew
in time	**rechtzeitig**	**rehkht**tsightikh
late	**spät**	shpait
midnight	**Mitternacht**	**mit**terrnahkht
noon	**Mittag**	**mit**targ
hour	**Stunde**	**shtun**der
minute	**Minute**	min**noo**ter
second	**Sekunde**	seh**kun**der
quarter of an hour	**Viertelstunde**	feerterl**shtun**der
half an hour	**halbe Stunde**	**hahl**ber **shtun**der

Days

What day is it today?	**Welchen Tag haben wir heute?**	**vehl**khern targ **har**bern veer **hoy**ter
Sunday	**Sonntag**	**zon**targ
Monday	**Montag**	**moan**targ
Tuesday	**Dienstag**	**deens**targ
Wednesday	**Mittwoch**	**mit**vokh
Thursday	**Donnerstag**	**don**nerrstarg
Friday	**Freitag**	**frigh**targ
Saturday	**Samstag/Sonnabend**	**zahms**targ/**zon**narbernt
in the morning	**am Morgen**	ahm **mor**gern
during the day	**tagsüber**	**targs**ewberr
in the afternoon	**am Nachmittag**	ahm **nahkh**mittarg
in the evening	**am Abend**	ahm **ar**bernt
at night	**nachts**	nahkhts
the day before yesterday	**vorgestern**	**foar**gehsterrn
yesterday	**gestern**	**geh**sterrn
today	**heute**	**hoy**ter
tomorrow	**morgen**	**mor**gern
the day after tomorrow	**übermorgen**	**ew**berrmorgern
the day before	**der vorhergehende Tag**	derr foar**havr**gayernder targ
the next day	**der Tag danach**	derr targ dah**narkh**
two days ago	**vor zwei Tagen**	foar tsvigh **tar**gern
in three days' time	**in drei Tagen**	in drigh **tar**gern
last week	**letzte Woche**	**leh**tster **vo**kher
next week	**nächste Woche**	**nehkh**ster **vo**kher
for two weeks	**zwei Wochen lang**	tsvigh **vo**khern lahng
birthday	**der Geburtstag**	derr ger**boorts**targ
day	**der Tag**	derr targ
day off	**der freie Tag**	derr **frigh**er targ
holiday	**der Feiertag**	derr **figh**errtarg
holidays	**die Ferien**	dee **fay**riern
month	**der Monat**	derr **moa**nart
school holidays	**die Schulferien**	dee **shool**fayriern
vacation	**der Urlaub**	derr **oor**lowp
week	**die Woche**	dee **vo**kher
weekday	**der Wochentag**	derr **vo**kherntarg
weekend	**das Wochenende**	dahss **vo**khernehnder
working day	**der Werktag**	derr **vehrk**targ

Months

January	**Januar**	**yah**nuarr
February	**Februar**	**fay**bruarr
March	**März**	mehrts
April	**April**	ah**pril**
May	**Mai**	migh
June	**Juni**	**yoo**ni
July	**Juli**	**yoo**li
August	**August**	ow**gust**
September	**September**	sehp**tehm**berr
October	**Oktober**	ok**toa**berr
November	**November**	noa**vehm**berr
December	**Dezember**	day**tsehm**berr
since June	**seit Juni**	zight **yoo**ni
during the month of August	**während des Monats August**	**vai**rernt dehss **moa**narts ow**gust**
last month	**im letzten Monat**	im **lehts**tern **moa**nart
next month	**im nächsten Monat**	im **nehkh**stern **moa**nart
the month before	**der vorhergehende Monat**	derr foar**hayr**gayernder **moa**nart
the month after	**der folgende Monat**	derr **fol**gernder **moa**nart
July 1	**der 1. Juli**	derr **ehr**ster **yoo**li
March 17	**der 17. März**	derr **zeept**saynter mehrts

Letter headings are written thus:

Munich, August 17, 1979	**München, 17. August 1979**
Dusseldorf, July 1, 1974	**Düsseldorf, 1. Juli 1979**

Seasons

spring	**der Frühling**	derr **frew**ling
summer	**der Sommer**	derr **som**merr
autumn	**der Herbst**	derr hehrpst
winter	**der Winter**	derr **vin**terr
in spring	**im Frühling**	im **frew**ling
during the summer	**während des Sommers**	**vai**rernt dehss **som**merrs
in autumn	**im Herbst**	im hehrpst
during the winter	**während des Winters**	**vai**rernt dehss **vin**terrs

REFERENCE SECTION

Public holidays

While there are additional regional holidays, only national holidays in Germany (D), Austria (A) or Switzerland (CH) are cited below.

Jan. 1	**Neujahr**	New Year's Day	D A CH
Jan. 2			CH*
Jan. 6	**Heilige 3 Könige**	Epiphany	A
May 1	**Tag der Arbeit**	Labour Day	D A
Aug. 15	**Mariä Himmelfahrt**	Assumption Day	A
Oct. 26	**Nationalfeiertag**	National Day	A
Aug. 1	**Nationalfeiertag**	National Day	CH
Nov. 1	**Allerheiligen**	All Saints' Day	A
Dec. 8	**Unbefleckte Empfängnis**	Immaculate Conception	A
Dec. 25	**1. Weihnachtstag**	Christmas Day	D A CH
Dec. 26	**2. Weihnachtstag**	St. Stephen's Day	D A CH*
Movable dates:	**Karfreitag**	Good Friday	D CH*
	Ostermontag	Easter Monday	D A CH
	Christi Himmelfahrt	Ascension	D A CH
	Pfingstmontag	Whit Monday	D A CH
	Fronleichnam	Corpus Christi	A

* Most cantons

The year round...

	Hamburg	Munich	Vienna	Zurich
January	35.6°F	33.8°F	33.8°F	35.6°F
February	37.4	37.4	37.4	41.0
March	46.4	48.2	46.4	50.0
April	55.4	57.2	57.2	59.0
May	64.4	64.4	66.2	66.2
June	71.6	69.8	71.6	73.4
July	73.4	73.4	77.0	77.0
August	73.4	73.4	75.2	75.2
September	66.2	68.0	68.0	68.0
October	55.4	55.4	57.2	57.2
November	44.6	44.6	44.6	44.6
December	39.2	35.6	37.4	37.4

Common abbreviations

ACS	**Automobil-Club der Schweiz**	Automobile Association of Switzerland
ADAC	**Allgemeiner Deutscher Automobil-Club**	General Automobile Association of Germany
a. M.	**am Main**	on the Main River
a. Rh.	**am Rhein**	on the Rhine River
AvD	**Automobil-Club von Deutschland**	Automobile Club of Germany
Bhf	**Bahnhof**	railway station
BRD	**Bundesrepublik Deutschland**	Federal Republic of Germany (West Germany)
DB	**Deutsche Bundesbahn**	Federal German Railway
DDR	**Deutsche Demokratische Republik**	German Democratic Republic (East Germany)
d. h.	**das heißt**	i.e. (that is)
DIN	**Deutsche Industrie-Norm**	German Industrial Standard
Frl.	**Fräulein**	Miss
G.	**Gasse**	lane
Hbf.	**Hauptbahnhof**	main railway station
Hr.	**Herr**	Mr.
LKW	**Lastkraftwagen**	lorry/truck
MEZ	**Mitteleuropäische Zeit**	Central European Time
Mio.	**Million**	million
Mrd.	**Milliarde**	1000 millions (billion)
n. Chr.	**nach Christus**	A. D.
ÖAMTC	**Österreichischer Automobil-Motorrad- und Touring-Club**	Austrian Automobile, Motorcycle and Touring Association
ÖBB	**Österreichische Bundesbahnen**	Austrian Federal Railways
PKW	**Personenkraftwagen**	motor car
Pl.	**Platz**	square
PS	**Pferdestärke**	horsepower
PTT	**Post, Telephon, Telegraph**	Post, Telephone and Telegraph Office
SBB	**Schweizerische Bundesbahnen**	Swiss Federal Railways
St.	**Stock**	floor
Str.	**Straße**	street
TCS	**Touring-Club der Schweiz**	Swiss Touring Club
usw.	**und so weiter**	etc.
v. Chr.	**vor Christus**	B. C.
z. B.	**zum Beispiel**	e.g. (for example)
z. Z.	**zur Zeit**	at present

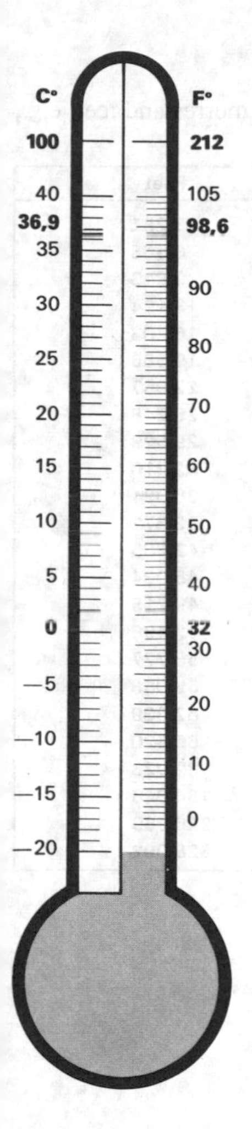

Conversion tables

Centimetres and inches

To change centimetres into inches, multiply by .39.

To change inches into centimetres, multiply by 2.54.

	in.	feet	yards
1 mm	0,039	0,003	0,001
1 cm	0,39	0,03	0,01
1 dm	3,94	0.32	0,10
1 m	39,40	3,28	1,09

	mm	cm	m
1 in.	26,4	2,54	0,025
1 ft.	304,8	30,48	0,304
1 yd.	914,4	91,44	0,914

(32 metres = 35 yards)

Temperature

To convert Centigrade into degrees Fahrenheit, multiply Centigrade by 1.8 and add 32.

To convert degrees Fahrenheit into Centigrade, subtract 32 from Fahrenheit and divide by 1.8.

Metres and feet

The figure in the middle stands for both metres and feet, e.g., 1 metre = 3.281 ft. and 1 foot = 0.30 m.

Metres		Feet
0.30	1	3.281
0.61	2	6.563
0.91	3	9.843
1.22	4	13.124
1.52	5	16.403
1.83	6	19.686
2.13	7	22.967
2.44	8	26.248
2.74	9	29.529
3.05	10	32.810
3.35	11	36.091
3.66	12	39.372
3.96	13	42.635
4.27	14	45.934
4.57	15	49.215
4.88	16	52.496
5.18	17	55.777
5.49	18	59.058
5.79	19	62.339
6.10	20	65.620
7.62	25	82.023
15.24	50	164.046
22.86	75	246.069
30.48	100	328.092

Other conversion charts

For	see page
Clothing sizes	115
Currency converter	136
Distance (miles-kilometres)	144
Fluid measures	142
Tire pressure	143

Weight conversion

The figure in the middle stands for both kilograms and pounds, e.g., 1 kilogram = 2.205 lb. and 1 pound = 0.45 kilograms.

Kilograms (kg.)		Avoirdupois pounds
0.45	**1**	2.205
0.90	**2**	4.405
1.35	**3**	6.614
1.80	**4**	8.818
2.25	**5**	11.023
2.70	**6**	13.227
3.15	**7**	15.432
3.60	**8**	17.636
4.05	**9**	19.840
4.50	**10**	22.045
6.75	**15**	33.068
9.00	**20**	44.889
11.25	**25**	55.113
22.50	**50**	110.225
33.75	**75**	105.338
45.00	**100**	220.450

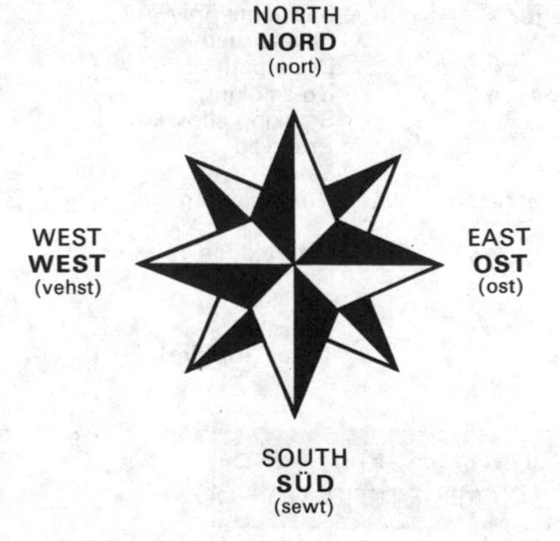

What does that sign mean?

Achtung	Caution
Aufzug	Lift (elevator)
Ausgang	Exit
Auskunft	Information
Ausverkauf	Sales
Ausverkauft	Sold out
Besetzt	Occupied
Bitte klingeln	Please ring
Drücken	Push
Eingang	Entrance
Eintreten ohne zu klopfen	Enter without knocking
Eintritt frei	No admission charge
Frei	Vacant
Für Unbefugte verboten	No trepassing
Gefahr	Danger
Geschlossen	Closed
Heiß	Hot
Kalt	Cold
Kasse	Cashier's
Kein Zutritt	No entrance
Lebensgefahr	Danger of death
Lift	Lift (elevator)
Nicht berühren	Do not touch
Nichtraucher	No smoking
Notausgang	Emergency exit
Nur für Anlieger	Residents only
Privatweg	Private road
Radweg	Cycle path
Rauchen verboten	No smoking
Raucher	Smoking allowed
Reserviert	Reserved
Schlußverkauf	Sales
Unbefugtes Betreten verboten	No trepassing
...verboten	...forbidden
Vorsicht	Caution
Ziehen	Pull
Zu verkaufen	For sale
Zu vermieten	To let (for hire)

VORSICHT, BISSIGER HUND
BEWARE OF THE DOG

Emergency

By the time the emergency is upon you it's too late to turn to this page to find the German for "I'll scream if you...". So have a look at this short list beforehand—and, if you want to be on the safe side, learn the expressions shown in capitals.

Be quick	**Schnell**	shnehl
Call the police	**Rufen Sie die Polizei**	**roo**fern zee dee poali**tsigh**
CAREFUL	**VORSICHT**	**foar**zikht
Come here	**Kommen Sie her**	**kom**mern zee hayr
Come in	**Herein**	heh**righn**
Fire	**Feuer**	**foy**err
Gas	**Gas**	gahss
Get a doctor	**Holen Sie einen Arzt**	**hoa**lern zee **igh**nern ahrtst
Go away	**Gehen Sie weg**	**gay**ern zee vehk
HELP	**HILFE**	**hil**fer
Get help quickly	**Holen Sie schnell Hilfe**	**hoa**lern zee shnehl **hil**fer
I'm ill	**Ich bin krank**	ikh bin krahnk
I'm lost	**Ich habe mich verrirt**	ikh **har**ber mikh feh**reert**
I've lost...	**Ich habe...verloren**	ikh **har**ber ... fehr**loa**rern
Keep your hands to yourself	**Hände weg**	**hehn**der vehk
Leave me alone	**Lassen Sie mich in Ruhe**	**lahs**sern zee mikh in **roo**er
Listen	**Hören Sie**	**hur**rern zee
Look	**Schauen Sie**	**show**ern zee
Look out	**Passen Sie auf**	**pahs**sern zee owf
POLICE	**POLIZEI**	poli**tsigh**
Quick	**Schnell**	shnehl
STOP	**HALT**	hahlt
Stop here	**Bleiben Sie hier stehen**	**bligh**bern zee heer **shtay**ern
Stop that man	**Haltet den Mann**	**hahl**tert dayn mahn
Stop thief	**Haltet den Dieb**	**hahl**tert dayn deep
Stop or I'll scream	**Halt oder ich schreie**	hahlt **oa**derr ikh **shrigh**er

FOR CAR ACCIDENTS, see page 150

Index

Abbreviations 184
Airport 65
Arrival 22
Baggage 24, 71
Ballet 82
Banks 134
Barber's 121
Basic expressions 15
Beach 87
Bill 31, 159
Body, parts of 163
Bookshop 104
Breakfast 34
Bus 73
Cables 138
Camping 89, 106
Car 142
  accident 150
  breakdown 151
  parts 152
  police 150
  rental 26
  repair 155
Casino 85
Change 25
Church services 79
Cinema 80
Clothes 112
Coach 73
Colours 113
Concerts 82
Customs control 23, 146
Dancing 84
Dating 95
Days 181
Dentist 172
Directions 187
Doctor 162
Drinks 58
Dry cleaning 126
Eating out 38
  appetizers 44
  cheese 55
  dessert 56
  drinks 58
  egg dishes 47
  fish and seafood 47
  fruit 55
  meat 50
  pasta, pizza 45
  sauces 53
  soups 45
  vegetables 54
Electrical appliances 119
Emergency 189
Expressways 147
Filling stations 142
Games 85
Grammar 7
Hairdressing 121
Hotel 25, 28
  checking in 29
  checking out 37
  difficulties 35
  registration 32
  service 33
Introductions 92
Invitations 94
Ladies' hairdressing 122
Laundry 126
Materials 114
Measurements

metric 130, 186
fluids 142
km/miles 144
sizes (clothing) 115
temperature 185
weight 130, 187
Medical section 162
Money 25, 134
Months 182
Motorways 147
Movies 80

Nationalities 174
News-stand 104
Night clubs 83
Numbers 175

Opera 82
Optician 173

Passport control 22, 146
Porters 24, 71
Post-office 137
Pronunciation 12
Provisions 129
Public holidays 183

Questions 78, 100, 144, 179

Railways 66
Records 120
Relaxing 80
Religious services 79
Road signs
international 160
national 149

Seasons 182
Shopping guide 97
bookshop 104
chemist's 108
clothing 112
colours 113
cosmetics 110
drugstore 108
dry cleaning 126
electrical appliances 119
hairdresser's 121
jeweller's 123
laundry 126
photography 127
provisions 129
records 120
shops, list of 98
tobacconist's 132
toiletry 110
Sightseeing 75
Signs and notices 188
Sizes 115
Snacks 64
Souvenirs 131
Sports 86
Stationer's 104
Subway 72

Taxis 27
Telegrams 138
Telephone 36, 139
Temperature 183, 185
Theatre 81
Time 178
Travel 65
bus 73
car 142
coach 73
plane 65
tickets 69
train 66
tram 73
Tire pressure 143

Underground 72

Voltage 119

Weather 93
Weight 187
Wine 59
Winter sports 88

Quick reference page

Here are some phrases and expressions which you'll probably need most frequently on your trip:

Please.	**Bitte.**	**bitt**er
Thank you.	**Danke schön.**	**dahng**ker shurn
Yes/No.	**Ja/Nein.**	yar/nighn
Excuse me.	**Verzeihung!**	fehr**tsigh**ung
Waiter, please!	**Herr Ober!**	hehr **oa**berr
How much is that?	**Wieviel macht es?**	vee**feel** mahkht ehss
Where are the toilets?	**Wo sind die Toiletten?**	voa zint dee toaah**leh**tern

WC/00/Toiletten	Toilets
 **Herren** (**heh**rern)	 **Damen** (**dar**mern)

Can you tell me...?	**Können Sie mir sagen...?**	**kur**nern zee meer **zar**gern
where/when/why	**wo/wann/warum**	voa/vahn/vah**rum**
Help me, please.	**Helfen Sie mir, bitte.**	**hehl**fern zee meer **bitt**er
Where is the... consulate?	**Wo ist das... Konsulat?**	voa ist dahss... konzoolaht
American	**amerikanische**	ahmehree**kar**neescher
British	**britische**	**brit**isher
Canadian	**kanadische**	kah**nah**deesher
What does this mean?	**Was bedeutet das?**	vahss ber**doy**tert dahss?
I don't understand.	**Ich verstehe nicht.**	ikh fehr**shtay**er nikht
Do you speak English?	**Sprechen Sie Englisch?**	**shpreh**khern zee **ehng**lish